BUILDING SCHOOLS FOR

1870-1914

The Victorian Society

THE VICTORIAN SOCIETY
in conjuction with

ald Print

© The Victorian Society 2012

Printed and published in association with The Victorian Society by:

ALD Design & Print
279 Sharrow Vale Road
Sheffield S11 8ZF
Telephone 0114 267 9402
E:mail a.lofthouse@btinternet.com

The Victorian Society
1 Priory Gardens
London
W4 1TT
www.victoriansociety.org.uk

ISBN 9781901587951

First published: September 2012

All rights reserved
No part of this publication may be reproduced, stored in a retrieval system or transmitted in any form or by any means, electronic, mechanical, photocopying, recording or otherwise, without the prior written permission of the publisher.

All views and comments printed in this book are those of the author and should not be attributed to the publisher.

In Memory of Jean Moulson

Victorian Society member

Langsett Road Board School, date label

CONTENTS

Foreword 1

Building Schools for Sheffield 3

The Buildings 7

The Leopold Street Buildings 11

Gazetteer
    Sheffield Schools 17
    The Township Schools 75

Appendix: Sheffield architects and their schools, 1870-1914 89

Select Bibliography 93

Acknowledgements 94

Foreword

This book is about the buildings constructed as state schools in Sheffield between 1870 and 1914, the period when elementary education became officially compulsory and universal. By Sheffield we mean not just the town, later city, of Sheffield as it existed at that time, but the city as defined by the boundaries set in 1974. So we record not only the schools built by the Sheffield School Board and its successor the Sheffield Education Committee, but also those for which school boards in surrounding townships, such as Norton and Handsworth, were then responsible, and which were later brought within the control of the Board and Council. Schools built before 1870 and after 1914 are not included; nor are those built during that period by organisations (such as churches) other than the school boards and the Sheffield Education Committee, nor those purchased as existing schools by those bodies.

We have set out to celebrate and draw attention to an important architectural heritage. Every town and city was obliged to ensure the provision of schooling for local children from 1870. The results, in architectural terms, were mixed. Sheffield, however, has one of the best collections outside London of schools of the period[1]. Moreover, of about 64 schools built in what is now the city between 1870 and 1914, 46 survive and 28 of them are still schools. Others are in other educational, community or commercial use. Only 14 have disappeared completely; sadly, 4 buildings currently languish unused and at risk. The historian of the Sheffield School Board, J H Bingham, writing in 1949, remarked 'if the members of the Board ever conjectured as to the future, they must have anticipated their reasonably well-designed and thoroughly well-built schools lasting for a couple of centuries'[2]. Such a prospect seems achievable for many of their schools. They are significant, often monumental, structures which were intended to make a social point and did so with great effect. Changing population patterns and evolving educational requirements caused the destruction of those schools which have been lost, but the buildings that remain deserve in our view to be better known and appreciated.

The book it is not about the story of education in Sheffield, though the context is of course important. The years 1870-1914 were among the most important in the city's educational history. They saw the establishment of clear expectations that a basic education was essential for everybody; and of an understanding and acceptance that it was the responsibility of local government to assess and meet needs, and of taxpayers both locally (through the rates) and nationally (through general taxation) to meet the costs. At first, the 1870 Education Act which mandated the new education system allowed the charging of modest fees to parents; 2d to 6d a week, with a remission scheme for the poorest families. By 1902 it had become obvious that even small fees acted as a deterrent to many and in that year they were abolished, bringing in a genuinely free and effective universal system of schooling. It then fell to the newly established Education Committee of the City Council to provide places for all the city's children.

---

[1] *Sheffield*, by Ruth Harman and John Minnis. Pevsner Architectural Guides, 2004

[2] *The Sheffield School Board*, by Alderman J H Bingham. Sheffield, J W Northend Ltd, 1949

In Sheffield, as elsewhere, education thinking had moved beyond compulsory, basic schooling. By the time the Sheffield School Board was abolished in 1903 it had created a system of elementary education supplemented by specialist technical secondary education for the brightest children regardless of their means. The School Board and the emerging University of Sheffield between them offered a comprehensive structure providing for infants through to undergraduates, and it was no accident that in the centre of Sheffield the necessary buildings were planned together. The buildings put up by the Board and the City Council reflected a very high level of civic pride and engagement. We hope that this record will introduce many people to a remarkable survival which still contributes to education in Sheffield and to the character of the city.

South Yorkshire Group
The Victorian Society

Building Schools for Sheffield

Like most towns and cities, Sheffield experienced a boom in school building in the period between the passing of Forster's Education Act in 1870, and the outbreak of the First World War. From 1870 until 1903, its schools were the responsibility of the School Board; thereafter, of the City Council, responsibility for the provision of education having been transferred to local authorities which set up education committees to exercise it. Schools were also built by the School Boards of surrounding townships which were later absorbed, partially, into the city: Ecclesfield, Grenoside, Handsworth, Eckington and Mosborough, Beighton and Norton. From a standing start in 1871 some 64 new schools were built in the area which now constitutes the city, together with substantial offices for the Sheffield School Board. The Sheffield School Board took pride in being the first such board in the country to start building a school.

Sheffield could not be immune from the pressure of rising population, particularly of school age, in the period. The town's population more than tripled between 1831 and 1871, to reach 239,000; then it expanded to 455,000 by 1911, partly by boundary extension. Much of the growth was in the younger age groups. There was no numerical shortage of schools in Sheffield in mid-19th century - there were over 150 of them - but they were mostly small. They ranged from charity, church and chapel schools and foundations like the former Wesleyan College (now King Edward VII School) through the Mechanics' Institute to private schools for the daughters of the well-off and dame schools for poor children, some of which were better at selling Factory Acts exemption certificates to parents, to allow their children to go to work, than at providing any education. As late as 1840 a local estimate suggested that barely a third of children got any schooling at all. The picture was probably not much different from that in other towns.

Nor could the city avoid the economic pressure for a better-educated - rather, an educated - working class. The quality and quantity of education provision was a national issue from the 1830s, when government finally gave in to political pressure and offered public money to the Anglican and non-conformist churches to set up and run schools. Grants were channelled through the National Society, which reflected Anglican interests, and the British and Foreign School Society, which was non-denominational in theory but largely dominated by non-conformist interests. Subsequent administrations struggled with the issue of how, if at all, to educate a rapidly rising population in an era of industrial expansion. From the 1840s, if not before, there were complaints that the Germans did it a lot better.

In well-established British fashion, successive governments tried to leave it to the voluntary sector, with the grant support just mentioned, and Factory Act provisions for at least part-time education for young employees; but this was limited to large factories - not then much of a feature of the Sheffield economy - and anyway much honoured in the breach. In the late 1860s the Liberal government pressed the National and British Societies to expand their operations to provide for the ever-growing population. They did not do so, and the consequence was Forster's Education Act of 1870 which was the framework within which Sheffield's education provision made an enormous leap forward.

Sheffield was one of the first adopters of the Act, holding elections for membership of its new School Board in November 1870. The election sparked great interest in the town, not least because each elector had fifteen votes, that being the number of seats to be filled. The membership of the first board demonstrated the interest of the industrial and commercial community in improving education, for those elected included, as well as Skelton Cole, a prominent draper, three leading steelmasters - Mark Firth, later founder of the University of Sheffield, Charles Doncaster, and Sir John Brown, engineer, who became the Board's first chairman. These men clearly influenced significantly the energetic way in which the Sheffield School Board set about its business.

Its initial work focused on the appointment of a clerk and a solicitor, the establishment of committees and the important task of estimating the demand in the town for school places which the Board would have to meet. This was not helped by the refusal of the Home Office to allow school boards access to census information without paying an amount the Sheffield Board thought far too high. Instead, the Sheffield police were asked to count the numbers of school-age children, and did so for less than a quarter of the Home Office's charge (but perhaps at a price in accuracy). The Board also found itself approached by the operators of numerous schools, notably denominational ones, offering premises for the Board's use. Some of these were taken up, mostly on a short-term basis. Its statutory role was to fill the gaps left by the voluntary schools; in practice the public sector eventually dominated provision.

By May 1871 the Board was ready to seek an architect to run its building programme, and an advertisement was duly placed in the local press: 'The Sheffield School Board are prepared to appoint a gentleman to act as Surveyor and Architect'. The duties included prospecting for suitable sites, negotiating their lease or purchase, and an annual inspection of the entire School Board estate, as well as designing new schools; the salary was £100 pa (that figure was halved in 1873 when a requirement to attend all board meetings was removed). It was of course assumed that the architect would take the usual 5% fee from the construction contracts.

The Board wanted to move rapidly. Applicants had only ten days to submit their bids, after which Board members balloted among the 15 applicants. The winner, after two rounds of voting, was C J (Charles John) Innocent (1839-1901) of Innocent and Brown, one of the handful of architects' practices then based in Sheffield. As will be seen, the choice was inspired. A young man - only 32 when appointed - Innocent clearly had the energy necessary to match the Board's. The relationship seems to have begun harmoniously enough; at any rate Innocent and Brown built 19 of the Board's first 21 schools. Innocent's school practice was not confined to the Sheffield Board; he also designed a board school at Killamarsh, and numerous private, mainly church or chapel, schools.

The first school begun by the Sheffield Board, and the first post-1870 Act school begun in the country, was Newhall in Attercliffe. Unfortunately for the Board's pride in its early start, strikes and other problems delayed its opening until January 1873. Yet from a 21st century perspective the speed of design and construction is nothing short of extraordinary. The rate of progress thereafter was equally impressive. By the end of 1875, five years into its life, the Board had opened no fewer than 14 schools; on a single day in 1874 it staged the official opening of 5. Within ten years 21 new schools had been opened, and from then until 1914 the growth and spread of the city can in part be tracked through the location of its new schools.

In addition the Board had built its own offices and in doing so contributed to the creation of a unique educational complex in the centre of Sheffield. From an early stage it planned a town centre site for both offices and a Central School which would offer a higher level of education for selected pupils drawn from the Board's other schools. A site was bought in

March 1876 and over the next twenty years filled with a number of well-designed office and education buildings. The Board, and Mark Firth who funded the eponymous College which later became the University of Sheffield, employed good architects. Firth engaged T J Flockton of Sheffield to build his college alongside the Board's offices, and the Board jointly commissioned Flockton and the London School Board's architect, E R Robson, to design its offices and Central Schools. Robson's services having been secured, some Board members clearly felt there was scope for making greater use of them. Moreover, there were signs of discontent with Innocent, perhaps because of the cost of his work. At any rate, in 1878 a planned competition for a new school at Heeley was abandoned in favour of commissioning Robson. The project for Brightside School was also awarded to him, and both schools opened in 1880.

In 1881 the Board decided to dispense with a contracted professional architect and instead expand the role of its Clerk of Works to cover supervision of the school estate. It also instituted competitions for all individual new schools. C J Innocent now practised on his own following Brown's early death; though deprived of his retainer he was free to tender for further schools, building a further six, and one extension, between 1883 and 1893. By then other Sheffield practices were winning business, notably those of J B Mitchell-Withers, Hemsoll and Paterson, and Holmes and Watson.

The Sheffield School Board was responsible, from a standing start, for providing more than 40 new schools over its 32 year existence, as well as the Education Offices, and many school extensions. In the city centre it had added to its Central Schools and offices an infants' school in Bow Street, in 1894, and a Pupil Teacher Centre, in Holly Street, in 1899. The Central Schools had been extended with the addition of Science Schools in 1894. By the end of the century the Leopold Street complex was providing education at every level from infant to university, as well as teacher training; and it is this which makes it unique.

The Board spent over £500,000 on land alone in its first decade - though that included the Leopold Street site. Between 1871 and 1903 it established school places for over 47,000 children, at a cost of almost £750,000. While this included the costs of taking over some existing schools to meet the need for places before new schools could be built, the majority of the money went into the building programme. The Board's legacy to Sheffield City Council, which assumed responsibility for schools in 1903, was therefore an impressive one. But the task was not complete. The continued growth of population and the inevitable expansion of the city's boundaries led to the construction by the Council of a further 12 schools between 1903 and 1910. The Council, like the Board, looked mainly to local firms to design them. Its first school was Nether Green, commissioned from Holmes and Watson by the School Board but completed after the Council took over. The Council's main contractors were Holmes and Watson, architects of five of the twelve, and W J Hale, responsible for 'Sheffield's most striking early 20th century architecture'[3] and a pupil of Innocent and Brown. Watson was commissioned in particular to design several special schools. But the appointment of the first city architect for Sheffield in 1908 soon took all school design work away from private practices, and High Wincobank School, 1910, was the last of them.

---

[3] *Sheffield*, by Ruth Harman and John Minnis. Pevsner Architectural Guides, 2004

By the outbreak of war in 1914, the Board and the City Council had taken over a number of schools provided by the School Boards of the townships surrounding Sheffield. Five schools, and one under construction, were transferred from the Norton and Handsworth Boards to Sheffield in 1901, when the city boundaries were first extended. The township boards were also abolished in 1903, their responsibilities divided between Sheffield and the adjacent county councils, Derbyshire and the West Riding, and some of their schools were also later absorbed into the city.

The Buildings

Sheffield's board and council schools were, and still are, a distinguished collection of buildings. The Board, and the Council after it, took a distinctive approach. Their schools and offices were almost all of local stone, much of it the immediately recognisable creamy sandstone from Stoke Hall in Derbyshire, that would increasingly be used in the city centre; for example in E W Mountford's Town Hall (1897). In Sheffield as in other towns, the school buildings were clearly designed to make a statement in their communities. Frequently large, of two or three storeys, they usually dominated their surroundings, especially areas of crowded, terraced workers' housing. The Board and its architects, and especially Innocent and Brown, did not shrink from placing the buildings where their impact would be maximised; on rising ground, if not on top of a hill – a feature assisted by the city's geography. Here was a means for the Board to impress on Sheffielders the social and economic importance of what went on inside the schools as well as to reflect their civic pride.

There was no uniform Board design. C J Innocent in particular was keen to explain that while all his schools were designed on 'the same leading principles', each was tailored to the characteristics of its own site. Given Sheffield's physical geography, the tailoring was an especially interesting exercise. The resulting buildings include some of the most interesting and ornate of the entire stock. As early as 1873 Innocent and Brown published a short book, 'Illustrations of public elementary schools erected for the Sheffield School Board'[4] to demonstrate what they had had in mind when they wrote of their desire for the 'picturesque grouping of parts rather than……a redundance of ornament or enrichment' and to provide for 'all these buildings such distinctive external features as should express the purposes and the means of their erection'. This did not mean absence of ornament; Innocent's schools mostly sport a marked quantity of carved decoration, not least the name and arms of the School Board. As to the standard of design, build and fitting out, this was sufficient to attract criticism. The Liberal MP David Chadwick, invited in 1875 to open a Sheffield school, asked 'How in the name of fortune the School Board have persuaded the ratepayers of Sheffield to tolerate their extravagance in spending £100,000 in the building of fourteen or fifteen schools as substantial as so many castles!'[5]. There was, however, little criticism in the local press, which continued to report the regular opening ceremonies in tones of respect and approval; and Sheffield's cost per place was less than in other major towns. Complaints from outside about school board extravagance continued, nevertheless, for years, with the National Society commenting as late as 1894 on the Sheffield Board's 'costly and magnificent buildings'.

No architect could have a free hand in designing a board school; nor could a school board give totally free rein to local or personal preferences or prejudices. Substantial requirements were laid down by central government via the Education Committee of the Privy Council, forerunner of the later Ministry and Department of Education. On its foundation in 1839, to support voluntary schools, the Committee had published a code of practice for school building. This was revised and reissued in 1870 to guide the new school boards in matters of layout, cost and technical specification. Innocent and Brown,

---

[4] Sheffield, published by the authors, 1873
[5] *Sheffield*, by Ruth Harman and John Minnis, p21

Science School Entrance, Orchard Lane

and all the other firms involved in the Sheffield programme, were expected to follow these specifications. The code did not however have much to say about style. Here, Innocent and Brown had a clear view. Their predominant style was, in their words, 'English Domestic Gothic'. This might have been regarded as a brave choice, given the prevailing use of Gothic for churches. Religion was inseparable from educational thinking at the time; board schools were seen by many as a challenge to the churches and chapels which had provided most elementary education hitherto, and as board schools began to open so the competition from denominational schools expanded. Some school boards were thought to have deliberately avoided anything that smacked of religious architecture, seeking instead a deliberately secular approach - as, for example, in London where a Queen Anne style was favoured. This appears not to have been an issue in Sheffield.

Alongside their house style, Innocent and Brown observed the Whitehall guidance, and prevailing educational theory. This, as well as strictly pragmatic constraints on staff budgets, encouraged designs which gave the head teacher views into all or most of the classrooms, grouped round a central hall, so that pupil teachers could be kept under observation. For the same reasons, interior partitioning was generally of wood panels topped with glazing. Innocent and Brown's most extreme example of this - perhaps influenced by E R Robson[6] - was at Huntsman's Gardens School, shaped like a horseshoe. Theory was also observed in the segregation of pupils, with separate entrances for boys, girls and infants, and separate classrooms for the latter (thought essential on account of the noise generated by small children). Into the 1880s all the schools featured, especially in the infants' departments, a gallery - a stepped arrangement which allowed the teachers full view of the pupils and which, if the desks were set in blocks, permitted two or more classes to be taught simultaneously. These have of course now disappeared. Ceilings were high and windows large, much importance being attached to adequate ventilation. Where space permitted there was generally a covered playshed outside. From 1876 the Board routinely added a caretaker's house; many of these survive, as often do the original boundary walls and sometimes the railings.

Whatever the theoretical context, and although cost pressures after 1881 dictated simpler design, the work of Innocent and Brown, and of Innocent alone, carries their trademarks: large window arches often encompassing double or triple windows, with stones laid in herringbone pattern in the upper portions above the glazed area, or in the gables; slender bell turrets; externally-expressed stair towers; a varied set of roof lines; the arms of the

---

[6] England's Schools, by Elain Harwood, p42. English Heritage, 2010.

School Board and its name and the date in small stone letters, below a string course or round an apsidal feature. These were not, by and large, adopted by the other firms who worked for the Sheffield Board, the Board's cartouche apart. E R Robson's two schools of 1880, in Brightside and at Heeley Bank, brought to Sheffield something of the Queen Anne style Robson had used so effectively and extensively in his work for the London School Board. The Sheffield architects working in the 1880s and 1890s tended in the same direction, for example with rectangular rather than arched windows. They perhaps took more literally than Robson himself his view that 'a school should look like a school……large towers........exaggerated gables, wrought iron ridge excrescences doomed to speedy decay…are all better avoided'. Many of the later schools (including some of Innocent's later commissions) were architecturally less distinguished – certainly less distinctive – perhaps through financial constraints; but there are exceptions, especially as new influences were felt in the later years of the period. W J Hale, architect in 1896 of Bole Hill School in Walkley, and in 1904 of Hammerton Street (Ouseburn Road) School in Darnall, clearly expressed in his work elements of the Arts and Crafts movement; the latter is a particularly rich example. Such continuity as can be seen through the entire period is mainly in the choice of materials; the Board stuck to local stone for its schools. So, mostly, did the Council, though a very small number were built in brick in the years just before the First World War.

How well did the buildings function as schools? It is difficult to judge, and modern standards are not relevant. From a strictly educational viewpoint they appear to have been no more and no less successful than any schools of the period. They were not without some defects as buildings, however. One Inspector of Schools complained bitterly in 1893 about the ventilation, and had been doing so for a decade: 'The Sheffield Board Schools, though handsome buildings, are with few exceptions so draughty that we have constantly to wear hats…..while we are inspecting them'. He did not comment on the effect on the occupants! Moreover the steps of the galleries they all boasted were used as seating, not as platforms for benches, to the detriment of pupil comfort. It took Whitehall intervention to calm the Board's irritation with these remarks. It is evident however that the Board went to considerable lengths to ensure their buildings functioned well.

Sheffield's schools were on the whole solidly built, and have survived remarkably well, though their interior features may sit uneasily with modern educational organisation. Enemy action in World War 2 inevitably caused damage, but no total loss. More recently, government's Building Schools for the Future programme has led to the abandonment of some older schools in favour of modern replacements, often close by (eg Ann's Grove, Heeley). The disused school buildings remain at risk unless alternative uses can be found. This has happened in some cases: thus Bole Hill School in Walkley is in community and commercial use, Burgoyne Road in Walkley is partly residential, Woodbourn Road in Attercliffe is a community centre, part of Manor School in City Road is earmarked for restaurant use. But the survival rate is good. In the conversion of the Leopold Street complex into a hotel, restaurants and bars Sheffield has been fortunate to acquire an excellent example of re-use to meet modern needs.

The Leopold Street Buildings

The Leopold Street Buildings © *Valerie Bayliss*

As noted in the introduction, there developed in Leopold Street in the fourth quarter of the nineteenth century a fine complex of education buildings. It is among Sheffield's largest concentrations of listed buildings.

The area occupied by the development was in the town centre but was until the mid-1870s a maze of small streets, poor-quality housing, workshops and industrial premises, including two small steel works and a gas works. The origins of its redevelopment lay in the decision of the Sheffield Town Council to undertake a major reshaping of the town centre in the 1870s and 1880s. This reshaping – planned largely, on behalf of the council, by Innocent and Brown - saw the cutting through of Leopold Street and the removal of numerous narrow thoroughfares; and, gradually, the construction of what we think of as the Victorian core of Sheffield.

The development was well-timed to match the desire of the Sheffield School Board to stop renting offices in the town and instead acquire its own accommodation, both for its regular meetings and for the expanding staff needed to meet administrative demands and the management of a rapidly-growing school estate. Early in 1876 the Board bought, for £17,000, a large amount of property in 'Bow Street, Church Street, Smith Street, Orchard Lane and Orchard Street', and shortly afterwards spent another £4300 on an adjoining site. Then it sold some of its land to the Town Council as a site for what became the line of Leopold Street, on the basis that the Council would bear the cost of making up this new road and transfer a small part of its own holding to the Board. This slightly complicated transaction, which consolidated the holdings of both bodies, was agreed in May 1876.

This land-buying initiative was decidedly confident given that at the time school boards lacked legal powers to pay for the building of offices; they could only finance schools. In the course of 1876, however, Sheffield and numerous other school boards successfully lobbied central government to add such powers to an education bill then going through Parliament; the necessary clause was drafted for the government by the Sheffield Board's legal adviser. So the gamble paid off and the Board was able to start the building work soon afterwards.

It had already taken steps to find a suitable architect for its town centre buildings, establishing a special committee to advise on this rather than leaving the task to its building committee. Sheffield's characteristically ambitious plans envisaged not only town centre offices but Central Schools offering higher-level education to 'deserving and clever pupils…..irrespective of class' drawn from the Board's other schools. At the same time plans were developing in Sheffield for the establishment of facilities for higher education, limited at the time to University of Cambridge extension lectures, which had proved very popular. It was not until 1877 that the Board actually sold on part of its land to Mark Firth (a School Board member) for £2750 as 'a site for his proposed University College buildings', but the transaction had clearly been planned much earlier.

From the outset, the Board was concerned to ensure that while the sale to Mark Firth would divide ownership, the entire site should be planned in a co-ordinated way. The buildings committee had recommended an open competition to find a suitable firm for the whole project, but the special committee thought otherwise. The Board noted that Firth had himself already appointed T J Flockton of the Sheffield practice of Flockton and Abbott as architect for the university college; it was mindful that 'it is desirable that the buildings should be harmonious in design'; and it noted that its special committee proposed the appointment of E R Robson, architect to the London School Board, to work alongside Flockton (Robson happened to be a personal friend of the Board's Secretary, J F Moss). The two, Flockton and Robson, were therefore 'conjointly commissioned to prepare plans for the Central Schools and Offices'. Work must have proceeded apace, for in June 1876 the Board approved plans for both offices and Central Schools, these having already undergone several revisions, and all this before the legal authority to invest was obtained. The Board was as energetic in developing in Leopold Street as it was in its school building programme as a whole.

Firth's college was completed, for £20,000, by November 1878 and formally opened by Prince Leopold, Queen Victoria's youngest son, in 1879; he gave his name to the street too. The Board offices and Central Schools, by the time they were finished and fitted out in 1880, cost over £69,000. This was not the end of the story, however, and other projects followed. By 1899 there were five buildings on the site which between them offered education to students from infant to university levels, as well as providing a home to the city's education administrators.

As with all the Board's buildings, materials and design across the site are of high quality. The statement the Board made here is perhaps less emphatic than at many of its hilltop schools, but the buildings would still have dominated their original environment. The complex preceded the late Victorian commercial developments in the area, though creation of the new street undoubtedly stimulated further building. The Sheffield Medical Institution, opposite the Board offices, opened in 1888 – adding to the concentration of education facilities – and the nearby Leopold Chambers offices in 1894. But the area behind Leopold Street only gradually lost its much smaller-scale development.

The architects achieved the harmony desired by the Board, without uniformity. The buildings throughout the site gain from the use of the same Huddersfield stone. In

Leopold Street itself, the provision of a stone arcade to link the offices and the Central Schools, and the use of a free Renaissance style throughout, maintains unity but permits substantial variation in design. Flockton and Robson's Board offices (now the Leopold Hotel) are of 3 ½ storeys, with an elegant central, pillared door above which is a slender oriel, its corbel captured in the broken pediment of the doorway; above it, twin chimneys flank an arched window. There is a decorative frieze above the second storey. The open balustrade is broken by large dormers to the attic floor.

The Sheffield School Board Offices

To the right of the offices is Firth College, again by Flockton and Robson, a simpler building originally of two storeys; a third was added by Flockton and Gibbs in 1892. Its main front on West Street is dominated by the central oriel above the elaborately-framed main door which has carved figures of Art and Science, by Onslow Ford, in the spandrels. Carved festoons are placed above and below the oriel. An open balustrade frames a central broken pediment. A 3-bay extension, added later, joined the College frontage to the Board's offices in Leopold Street. Above, twin chimneys flank an arched window. A hall (now gone) was added on the West Street side in the 1930s.

To the left of the offices, beyond the linking arcade, are the Central Schools, Flockton and Robson's third and last building on the site. On the corner of Orchard Lane canted sections frame a small bow-fronted stretch with pilasters, arched pediment and blank cartouche. The corner front has a variety of carved features, the SBS logo among them. In Orchard Lane are separate doorways for boys and girls along the plain elevation of 2 ½ floors, set back to provide light for the basement. On top of the classrooms is a large hall, open to the roof inside and expressed externally via an end gable sporting massive twin chimneys enclosing an arched window, bigger cousin of the one over the Board's offices. Beyond is J B Mitchell-Withers' Science School extension of 1895, a deceptively small frontage for a large block running back parallel with Leopold Street.

The Board's coat of arms on the Central Schools, Leopold Street

The Central Schools, Leopold Street frontage

Firth College

The Board had by now added, in 1894, the Bow Street School, for 503 infants, and again by Mitchell-Withers. In 'stripped Classical' style, it is much the plainest of the Leopold Street buildings, its only decoration a series of pilasters. The original balustrade has gone, as has the original rooftop playground, but the simple pedimented bell turret remains. At £37 11s 8d per place it was by far the most expensive of the Board's schools, possibly because of the price of the land.

Finally, the Board added in 1899, adjoining the infants' school, the Holly Street Pupil Teachers Centre by H W Lockwood of Sheffield. Its symmetrical frontage combines bay-windowed stair turrets and rectangular windows, some topped by arches filled with decorative carving. The central doorway is set in a wide bay of slender mullioned windows beneath a carved solid balustrade; the building's name carved in elaborate letters over foliage. It contained three classrooms and ancillary rooms.

Bow Street Infants' School

The various schools underwent numerous changes in character over the years; eventually all were moved out of the centre, leaving the complex as purely council office accommodation. In the twentieth century there were additions, mainly of poor quality, in the courtyard. These were all swept away in the impressive restoration of the early 2000s which have refurbished the complex for residential, hotel and restaurant use.

Holly Street Teachers Centre

GAZETTEER

The gazetteer first lists all the schools built by the Sheffield School Board between 1871 and 1903, and then those built by the Sheffield Education Committee up to 1914, in the order in which they were formally opened. In the early years this was usually on the same day as they opened for enrolment; later on there was usually a gap, sometimes of months, between the practical and formal openings.

Then there is a section about the township school boards and the schools they built, followed by descriptions of many, but not all, of those that survive.

For each school the present street address is given except in the few cases where the street no longer exists. This is followed by the year of construction of each part of the school, and the architect, where known.

The surviving buildings are illustrated in colour. Black and white (either a photograph or the architects' drawing) indicates a building that no longer exists.

All colour images are © Alex Ekins unless otherwise indicated.

Newhall Board School

Sanderson Street S9
1873 and 1877, Innocent and Brown; 1886-9, C J Innocent; 1895
1906, Holmes and Watson

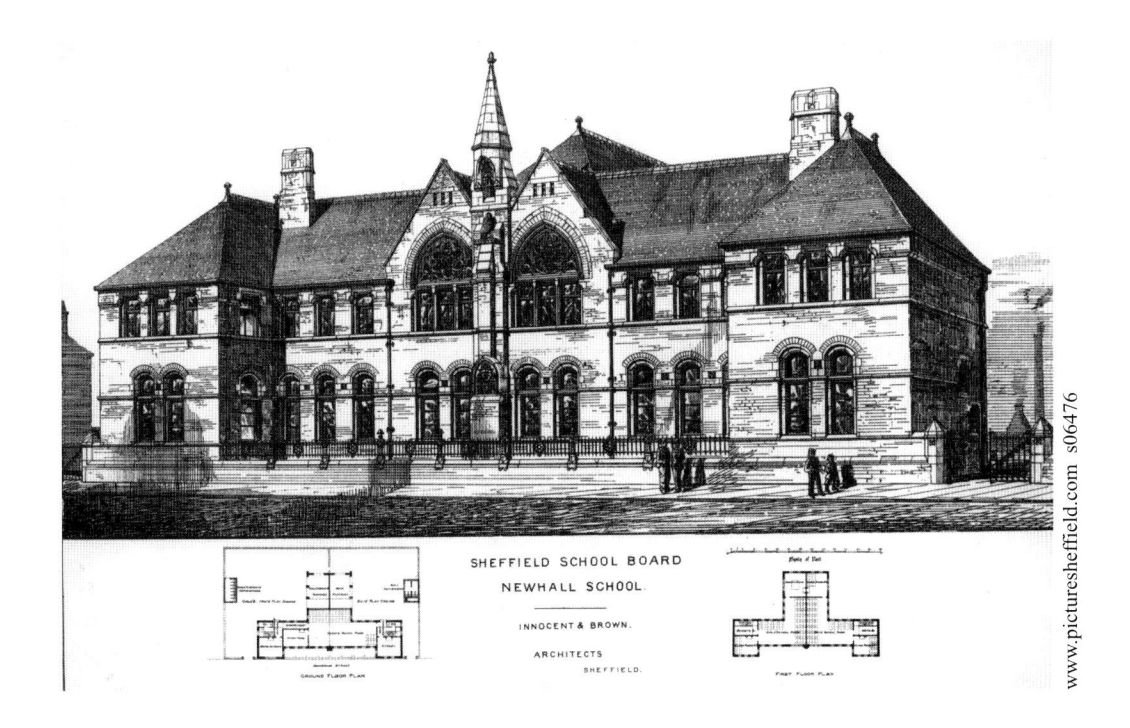

The first school opened by the Sheffield Board. The local press report noted the site was chosen 'not for its pleasant out-look, but because it is in the midst of a dense and ever-increasing population'. 6000 people lived in insanitary conditions on undrained land on the flood plain of the River Don; typhoid fever and epidemics of skin diseases were common. The need for education in such a district was paramount. The 600 places proved insufficient, and successive extensions brought numbers to 1596 by 1895. In 1907 a special school, by A F Watson, was added near the main one; the entire site covered an acre.

The constant pressure on capacity, and the need to build extensions, was to become a common experience for the Board. Newhall set another pattern: the use of by the architects, through the 19 schools they built for the Board, of elaborate styling – here Renaissance, elsewhere English Domestic Gothic. It was part of the clear policy to develop 'statement' buildings. Like all Innocent and Brown's schools, Newhall was of stone with slate roofs, the layout reflecting the latest educational thinking with a big central schoolroom or hall and ten classrooms around it, the interior divisions of timber with glazing above. A special feature of the 1895 extension here was a completely new system of mechanical ventilation which passed smoky air from outside through a screen, purified it and propelled it into the classrooms. The heating system was designed to keep the rooms at a constant 60 degrees even in the coldest weather.

Newhall was closed in 1970, the population of the district having diminished through slum clearance, and the school subsequently demolished.

Broomhill Board School
Beech Hill Road S10 2SA
1873, 1877, 1880, 1890, Innocent and Brown

The longest surviving of the architects' schools; the second opened by the Board; and the smallest it commissioned in its early days. Initially for 326 children, which the *Sheffield Independent* thought quite enough for local needs, the school was badly overcrowded from the start. Pressure for expansion, for example by enclosing the covered play areas, was constant; by 1890 there were places for 711. It cost in all £8929, including the (surviving) caretaker's house. Broomhill now offers 120 places for infants, a good example of changing standards.

The small site was on a quiet private road; the Board was obliged in 1874 to meet a share of the charges of adoption. It was built of Dunford Hill stone, with Handsworth ashlar dressings and a blue Welsh slate roof capped with red Berkshire ridge tiles, in what the *Independent* called 'the geometric style of Gothic architecture'. L shaped, it had a small bell tower (now gone) over the angle, and Innocent's usual covered open-sided playsheds, one surviving largely unaltered. The separate entrances for boys, girls and infants all survive, as does an original gatepost marked 'Girls and Infants'. There was a single classroom for each group, and the infants' room originally had a gallery. A major feature is the staircase tower, externally expressed as a strong curved corner to the building and dating from the 1890 extension. It later provided access to the rooftop playground created in 1943 after a fire destroyed the original roof and the second floor, which was not replaced. The street front boasts a fine array of windows, segment-headed on the ground floor; above, triplet windows are framed by large gables with trefoil heads; the return and rear facades are simpler, but still with some trefoil heads. There is the usual School Board cartouche and the Board's name on a string course.

Some original interior features survive, including some fine pine roof-beams.

Netherthorpe Board School
Netherthorpe Street S3 7JA
1873, 1878, Innocent and Brown; 1883-4, Innocent
Listed Grade 2

2000 square yards of land were purchased from John Hoyle to build the school, which with the later extensions cost over £13,000. It opened on 13 October 1873, with provision for 959 scholars; the extension took capacity to 1031. The local press reported that 'everything appears to have been most carefully designed in the most substantial and suitable manner'. The handsome solidity of the building still supports that comment. Built in the architects' characteristic Gothic Revival style, of squared stone with ashlar dressings, it is T-shaped and on 2 storeys. The symmetrical main elevation has a large central gable with first floor window arches encompassing lancet windows beneath stone tracery; ground floor windows below are round-headed triplets. A distinctive feature of this facade are the curved stair turrets, and the projecting, matching end wings with, again, large traceried window arches to the first floor at both front and rear. The original boys' entrance has been converted into a window recently but the carved stone surround and inscription survive. On the front gable the Sheffield School Board crest and the words 'Sheffield School Board 1873' remain, though slightly damaged. The interior has been much altered to make it fully accessible.

The rear wing is simpler. The roof was of slate, now waterproofed with a grey composition. Windows on both floors are double, rectangular above, segment-headed below.

The covered play shed, high boundary walls and some of the original railings survive, with two wrought iron gates; so does the caretaker's house in Dover Street. The double desks, to the patented design of the Board's secretary J F Moss, do not!

Philadelphia Board School
West Don Street S6 3BH
1873, 1877, 1886-7, Innocent and Brown; 1888, C J Innocent

Built to serve a heavily industrialised area in the Don Valley, north-west of the city centre, and to take 747 scholars. Two extensions raised the capacity to 1199, and added a caretaker's house.

In style Philadelphia reflected the architects' broad general approach. But it was a good example of their ability to vary both the external appearance and the detail of their schools. While West Don Street displayed many their trademarks (large arched gable-end windows with herringbone infill, roof gablets and double chimneys with ventilator outlets between them) it also featured an intriguing stepped arrangement of the windows in the wings at either end of the building. Yet overall it was markedly more regular in design than many of their schools.

The T-shaped, symmetrical building occupied two storeys, with separate halves for girls and boys. Older pupils used the first floor, with infants below. Girls shared the infants' playground, and a kitchen and manager's office occupied the wings. The school cost £14,290, including the extensions, fittings and caretaker's house.

Philadelphia closed in 1972 as the local population had declined significantly with housing clearance. It was later demolished.

Attercliffe Board School
Baldwin Street S2
1874 and 1877, Innocent and Brown; 1888-9

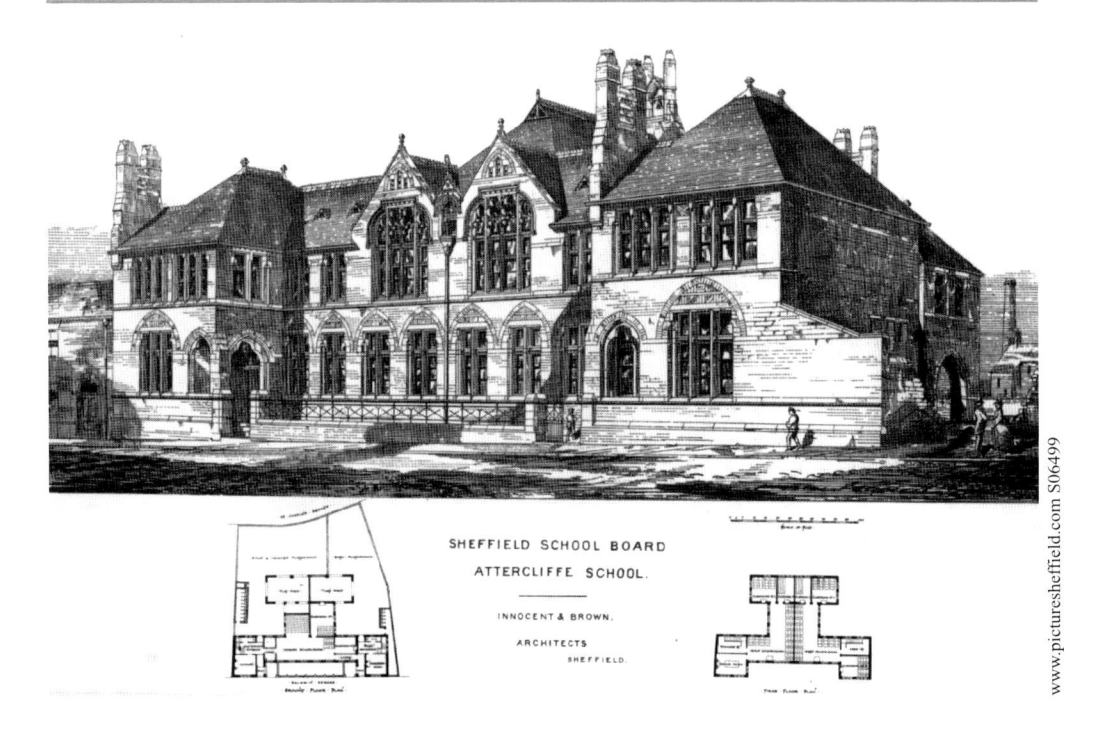

One of the numerous schools the Board had to provide for the dense population of the heavily industrialised Attercliffe district. As was becoming common, the original accommodation for 734 pupils had to be increased, to 779 in 1879 and 805 by 1889. But it was one of the cheapest in outlay per head.

The building had obvious similarities with Newhall, also in Attercliffe and opened seven months earlier. Of two storeys with a slate roof, it had two central pointed gables to the front elevation with chimneys, a bell tower and pavilion style staircase wings on either side. Each half of the school contained two large schoolrooms running front to back with two smaller classrooms leading off at the rear. A sewing room for the girls and a third classroom for the boys led off the main room at the front into the pavilion wings. Infants were accommodated on the ground floor to avoid steps. A manager's room and a kitchen were also provided on the ground floor. Separate entrances and playgrounds were provided for boys and girls, with covered play sheds for both. A caretaker's house was added in 1876-77 and the school enlarged for the infants in the 1880s.

Like Newhall the population using the school went into sharp decline after 1945 and closure was followed by demolition.

Carbrook Board School
Attercliffe Common S9 2AG
1874, 1877, Innocent and Brown; 1889, Innocent; 1900
Listed Grade 2

The school was opened in 1874, for 791 pupils, a further response to heavy industrial development in the Don Valley and the consequent provision of terraced housing for the workers; so the school catered for growing need. Its size was an issue from the outset. The Board had rapidly to seek Whitehall approval for extra places, which did not go down well; and it was pressed frequently by local interests to provide even more. In the event extension was delayed until 1889, when a second school (now demolished) for 600 boys and girls was built adjacent to the first. In 1899 the open, arcaded play areas of the first school were enclosed to form extra classrooms; by 1900 Carbrook housed 1477 children. A caretaker's house had been added in 1877.

The 1874 school, now a hotel, is of honey-coloured stone with ashlar dressings and slate roof. Two-storey, and a symmetrical H in plan, it presents a rather 'ecclesiastical' frontage to Attercliffe Common. This elevation has three gables, the central and largest flanked by buttresses and featuring two pointed-arch recesses, each enclosing triplet cusped lancets. Topping the gable is an octagonal turret with spire and finial, beneath them an elaborate arched niche and the SBS cartouche. Beneath the recesses the lower stages of the buttresses enclose plainer windows, both arched and rectangular; between the two storeys a band of Innocent and Brown's favourite stone herringbone work underlines the Board's name and date. The side gables surmount arched lancet windows on the first floor, with plain windows below. Buttresses on the corners, to ground floor only. Elsewhere, windows are plainer, shouldered rectangles. Evidence remains of the arched play areas. The rear corners of the front wing retain cloister-like porches with cusped arches and buttress. The original front walls, gateposts and railings survive.

Crookesmoor Board School
Oxford Street and Tay Street S6 3FP
1874, 1877 and 1881, Innocent and Brown; 1887, C J Innocent
Listed Grade 2

The Board spent £900 on the almost triangular site of 2100 square yards (purchased from the Sheffield Waterworks Company), and a further £6390 on the building, making a total of £7290; later extensions brought the total to over £19,000. The 1874 building, on Oxford Street, is a handsome Gothic Revival structure of cream local stone with slate roofs. A modified T in shape, it operated at first as two virtually identical schools. Girls and infants were accommodated together, with a shared playground and conveniences, but separate classrooms, while the boys were accommodated completely separately with an entrance from Tay Street. The front elevation, sadly compromised by a modern addition, features an elaborate version of the Board's cartouche, flanked by owl supporters, as part of a stone rainwater head. Ground floor windows are surmounted by cusped arches, first floor windows are arranged in triplets beneath arches, the central one traceried. Between the floors an ornamental band gives the Board's name and the date. There is a square wooden bell turret with fish-scale slates and a wooden finial, and a massive and complex chimney stack. The school had space for 779 pupils.

Innocent's 1881 extension is simpler but in broadly similar style with a hipped roof and square bell turret. It included provision for a further 395 boys, bringing total capacity to 1495.

Some original railings survive, and are listed along with the boundary walls and caretaker's house as well as the school itself. The school closed in 1994; it was used by the Connexions (youth and careers advice) Service but is now empty.

Lowfield Board School

London Road S2 4NJ
1874 and 1877-8, Innocent and Brown
Listed Grade 2

Lowfield was built for 705 pupils, but enlarged in 1879 to accommodate 785 (305 boys, 220 girls and 260 infants). It differs from the Board's other early schools in being single storey. What the *Sheffield City* Pevsner Guide describes as two 'well detailed Gothic style buildings' occupy a somewhat restricted site at a junction of two major roads leading into the city, with frontages to both. The larger, older building on London Road has attics above its single storey. It is angled to follow the line of the roads and a circular feature neatly links its two wings. Further along, a square tower with fishtail-tiled bell turret sits alongside the major arched gable end which contains the Board's usual coat of arms, name and the 1874 date. At the end of this elevation is the 1877 caretaker's house, integrated into the original structure. The later building on Queen's Road is similar in style, with a large main gable.

Windows in both buildings are mainly cusped, often lancet with transoms, and the architects' trademark herringbone stone work fills the gable ends. The original walls and some railings survive. Severe damage in the last War was well repaired.

Lowfield Community Primary school now caters for 214 pupils. Terraced housing next to the school was demolished in the 1980s, allowing space for a modern extension in great contrast to the original school, and using structural insulated panels on the roof to ensure energy efficiency.

Walkley Board School

Greaves Street (now Burnaby Crescent) S6 2RZ
1874 and 1877, Innocent and Brown, listed Grade 2; 1907, Hemsoll and Paterson

The first Board school in Walkley, it opened in 1874 with space for 779 elementary pupils, but attracted far more enrolments. A caretaker's house was built and the playground enlarged in 1876-1877. The 1907 addition was a 400 place infants' school on the other side of Greaves Street.

The listed 1874 building is characteristic Innocent and Brown; Gothic Revival, rock-faced stone with ashlar dressings. Almost monumental in conception, and dominating its hilltop, it is 2-storeyed and a broad H in shape, with a main range and cross-wings, all of them architecturally distinct. The large gable on the south-east facade contains a niche and inscribed band carrying the Board's usual arms, name and date. Above, two pairs of arched windows with cusped heads; above them, the string course forms arches. The gable rises into a bell turret beneath a substantial spire. The lower cross-wing has large ground floor window arches; the main range has 3 through-eaves dormers each with twin-light windows with arched heads beneath ventilator slits. The decorative ridge tiles survive, as do most of the original boundary walls. The building was of high quality but cost the Board less than £9000 and was one of its cheapest in cost per place terms. Empty and derelict for years, it has now been converted into student housing.

The 1907 infants' department, across the road, is a simpler Renaissance-style affair, the main range single storey with two gabled cross-wings, and shorter two-storey end ranges at right angles. From the main range roof rises a large open-centred Flemish gable. The south-east end range has an octagonal and domed bell turret. The building, with substantial modern extensions, is still a primary school.

Darnall Road Board School
Darnall Road S9
1875, Innocent and Brown; 1892, Innocent
Listed Grade 2

The school was built to serve the growing population of Darnall. Formerly a working class village of coal miners and hand forgers of pens and pocket knives, by the 1870s it housed the much-expanded Sanderson's steelworks and Craven's Railway Carriage and Waggon Works. Much of the accompanying terraced housing survives alongside modern development.

The gently sloping site for the school was beautifully exploited by the architects. The 1 and 1 ½ storey Domestic Gothic school, of coursed stone with ashlar dressings, has an asymmetrical long elevation onto the street. Towards the upper end of the range two substantial gables reflect the classrooms within. The lower end terminates in a projecting entrance block, a narrow, stone-capped bell-tower - effectively an extended buttress - with arched bell recess, then a single gable and an elegant apse, built up from the downward slope. Around the apse an inscribed decorative band announces the Board's name and the construction date (the SBS cartouche is on the front-facing elevation of the bell-tower buttress). The three gables contain different combinations of tall pointed arches enclosing cusped lancet windows. The hipped and gabled slate roof has decorated ridge tiles.

© Valerie Bayliss

In 1892 a single storey extension, linked by a curved wall, was added, as was a separate and larger building at the bottom of the school yard. This was of the same stone, simpler in style but with gables, inset arches and its own bell turret. Most of the original front walls survive. The caretaker's house was added in 1902, by which time the school offered 1267 places and had cost the Board over £19,000.

The building is currently in community education and local authority use.

Park Board School
Norwich Street S2 5PN
1875, Innocent and Brown; 1892 and 1900, C J Innocent

Park was close to the city centre and served an area of high density back to back housing, much of it built around courts.

An imposing two- and three-storey building, originally accommodating 752 pupils, it was re-arranged in 1880 to accommodate 802 and enlarged again in 1892 when a separate department for 370 boys, fronting on to Gilbert Street, was opened. This new department had a large room and four smaller rooms divided by moveable glass partitions designed by the architect, allowing flexibility in the utilisation of space. The previous boys' department was re-arranged, additional classrooms were added and it became a junior mixed department. The extra accommodation was necessary as other, voluntary sector and church schools in the Park area were full and children were constantly being refused admission. By this time Park School served 1,252 pupils. In 1899 approval was sought to provide additional accommodation for 120 infants, a room for cookery and laundry work and a caretaker's house.

Re-organised in 1954 as a junior and infant school, Park was soon overwhelmed by the formidable post war structures of Duke Street and Hyde Park flats. It was demolished in 1967.

Grimesthorpe Board School
Earl Marshal Road S4 4SB
1875, 1877, Innocent and Brown
Listed Grade 2

©Mary Howson

Grimesthorpe was opened officially in June 1875 by Sir John Brown, chairman of the Sheffield School Board; it was the Board's twelfth school. The initial capacity was 757 boys and girls, but that rose to 820 by 1889 through minor alterations and extensions. A caretaker's house was built in 1877. The school served what had been a village whose population was heavily involved in scissor making and grinding but which was overtaken by the development of industry in the Don Valley from mid-19th century; much of the associated late Victorian housing survives. In total some £9000 was spent on the school by the Board, including site purchase, fitting-out and extensions.

This was one of Innocent and Brown's more striking designs. On a very small, sloping corner site they devised a 2-storey-plus-basement building in Gothic Revival style, rather French in character and more dramatic than much of their English Domestic Gothic. Of coarse squared stone with ashlar dressings, it has tall gables and a slate roof with gablet ventilators and decorative ridge tiles. The plan is an H with an extended central transept leading to hexagonal wings sporting thin pointed buttresses. One buttress has a bellcote and lancet opening with octagonal spire and finial. There is abundant use of sill bands and lancet windows throughout. The bricked-up arches on the south and west sides were probably covered play areas. The original playground walls survive, their external semi-buttresses adding to the robust impression. On the south side of the building, the usual carved SSB cartouche is dated 1874.

The school closed in 1973 after serving a variety of age groups at different times, but the building remains in educational use.

Pye Bank Board School
Andover Street S3 9EG
1875, 1877, Innocent and Brown; 1884, Innocent
Listed Grade 2

Built at an eventual cost of £16,500, Pye Bank served the working-class housing crammed into Pitsmoor. The caretaker's house, of the standard Board design, was added on the Fox Street side in 1877. Innocent's 1884 extension increased capacity from 900 to 1497. The corner site, crowning a steep hill, is spectacular; on its opening it was called 'the highest, driest and coldest part of Sheffield', a 'handsome new school fixed like an eagle's eyrie'. Its clean new stone would have been a sharp contrast with the smoke-blackened housing around it.

The design, worthy of the site, is typical of the architects' Gothic Revival: T-shaped with added rear wings, and of two storeys, of coursed stone and ashlar dressings, and gabled and hipped slate roof. The formal main front on Andover Street (now providing an unimpeded view over the city but originally facing houses) has a projecting centre section with at ground floor 2 pairs of pointed-arch recesses divided by a buttress, and containing lancet windows. Above, a large arched recess encloses 2 shouldered lancet windows; above the recess, in a central quatrefoil, is the SBS cartouche, with the head of Minerva and local symbols. She is beneath an anvil and flanked by crossed daggers and an elephant, whose ivory was used for knife handles, and a cannon. Between the two storeys is the usual stone band labelled 'Sheffield School Board' and dated 1875. The central projection is contained by matching stair turrets. Elsewhere the finish is plainer with a mix of cusped, round-arched and shouldered windows. The front gate has disappeared, as have most of the cast-iron railings of the front wall; elsewhere, the high stone boundary walls remain.

The school survived successive housing redevelopments in the 1950s and 60s. Latterly a nursery and infant school, it was closed in 1990; the building is currently unused.

Springfield Board School

Broomspring Lane S10 2FA
1875, Innocent and Brown; 1892 and 1897, C J Innocent
Listed Grade 2

Springfield, considered at its opening as 'without exception the most handsome block of buildings the board have erected', initially offered 725 places but was extended within four years to 833. Another 515 were added in 1891-2 and 159, for infants, in 1896-7, making a total of 1490; a doubling in size in twenty years. The Board spent over £24,000, its second highest spend aside from the Central Schools. Springfield primary and nursery schools now serve an inner-city population; much of the original Victorian terraced housing has been replaced, successively, by brutalist 1960s flats and in the 1980s by housing on a more human scale.

The *Sheffield City* Pevsner calls the school 'a particularly impressive 3 storey example' of the architects' work. It bears many of their trademarks, exuberantly expressed. English Domestic Gothic, of rock-faced stone in courses and with ashlar dressings, beneath slate roofs with hips and gables. The usual separate entrances for boys, girls and infants, and infants alone, the latter dated 1897. The main block has 9 bays and 3 floors, the centre recessed; to one side is a slender bell turret. Ground floor windows are single-light; above, many windows are lancets enclosed in moulded arches whose tops are filled with stone slabs laid in herringbone pattern. In the top floor of the stair turret, a row of quatrefoil windows echo similar quatrefoils in some of the biggest arched windows. On the side wall is a fine example of the School Board cartouche and date label, enclosed in a pillared niche. The 1897 single-story extension onto Bolton Street has similar features.

At the rear a two storey building provided play space, the upper floor open-sided with iron railings. The original boundary walls and railings survive.

Manor Board School
Manor Lane S2 1TR
1876, Innocent and Brown, listed Grade 2
1889, Wightman and Wightman; 1907, Charles Hadfield

1876 building

The school's three buildings are ranged one behind another across the hillside off Manor Lane. The 1876 school is single storey, with a basement, of rock-faced stone, with long slate roof and decorative ridge tiles, a central fleche and tall triple chimneys; from the centre, a smaller gable rises from two buttresses. The west end gable of the cross range contains a large arch with double tall lancets flanked by smaller shouldered-arch windows. The cartouche between the lancets, with the standard SBS device and date, is in very good condition. At the east end is the integrated two-storey teacher's house (one of only two such provided by the School Board, apparently because local housing at the time was thought unlikely to attract the class of person sought as teacher). It has a front bay window with shoulder-arched openings, and a good mullioned first-floor window. The school's entrances are at the back, but on City Road the original railings survive, with here and in Manor Lane the inscribed gateposts for boys, girls' and infants' entrances. The building is unused but planned to become a restaurant.

The 1889 building was replaced with post-war structures, now sadly derelict. Behind them is Hadfield's 1907 extension, a 3 bay single-storey range backed by a hall. The bays are topped by heavy Flemish gables enclosing arched windows. At each end is a tall doorway with round-headed pediment, rather baroque in style, marked 'Boys' and 'Girls' respectively. Here and on the surviving gateposts, the lettering is in Arts and Crafts style. The 1907 date appears in a window arch keystone beneath a Flemish gable. A single-storey modern extension obscures the east frontage. A new primary school has been added to the rear.

1907 building © Valerie Bayliss

Fulwood Board School
David Lane, S10 4PH
1878, Innocent and Brown

The architects' simplest commission for the Board, and essentially a stone-built village school. Single-storey and rectangular, it has one projecting end gable facing the road. The two-storey schoolmaster's house at the other end of the range provides in effect a matching gable; between, barge-boarded gablets top the windows. These are tall and rectangular, with simple stone lintels. The slate roof supports two cylindrical witch's-hat ventilators on the cross-range. The bay-windowed house is L shaped, its end gables barge-boarded like the school, and with substantial stone chimneys. The low boundary walls and gateposts survive. So does the covered playshed which serves both the segregated playgrounds; its cast iron columns support a single roof which straddles the dividing wall.

This was the second of the two schools for which the Board provided a teacher's house, as the location was (and remains) relatively isolated; where did the 131 children provided for actually come from?

The building is now a local authority environmental studies centre, but under threat of closure.

Langsett Road Board School
Burton Street S6 2HH
1879, Innocent and Brown; 1888, Wightman and Wightman

The school was opened in 1879, to accommodate 960 pupils; there was a building for boys, and one for girls and infants, together with a playshed and caretaker's house. The 1888 addition was for 350 places for juniors, and thereafter the school taught on a mixed basis up to age 9, and boys and girls separately. The total cost of the school was £14,795.

The 1879 buildings, of darkish stone relieved by ashlar, are side by side. One is marked 'Sheffield School Board 1879", in a cusped niche over an elegant loggia sheltering the door. This block has stone mock barge-boards in the gables, flat-headed windows with stone lintels and stone string course; the main range appears to have contained a hall, and there are two through gable-ended wings on one side, one on the other, and an end cross wing. The second building has a recessed front with 2 projecting end wings; in the centre, a rather Jacobean shouldered gable with elaborate leaf carving within it and dripstone beneath. The 1888 addition at the rear of the site is a long 1 and 1½ floor range with gabled cross wings onto the yard. The Capel Street elevation has three small plain gables. Many of the buildings' decorative ridge tiles remain, along with various striking finials, as do some boundary walls and marked gateposts.

The area was originally terraced housing, but it is now mixed light industry/warehousing, and the school closed in 1976 following housing clearance. After two decades as the Langsett Music School it was abandoned in 1995 for demolition, but saved and is now in community use.

Heeley Bank Board School
Heeley Bank Road S2 3GL
1880, E R Robson
Listed Grade 2

E R Robson, architect to the London School Board, was a major player in board school design, probably the best known architect of board schools in England, and the only London architect to work for the Sheffield Board. This is one of his two Sheffield suburban schools.

Heeley Bank lasted as a school for almost exactly 100 years, opening in 1880 and closing as a school in 1980. Accommodating 900 pupils at a cost of £12,881, it provides a dramatic view on rising land and is instantly recognisable by the distinctive massive rear chimney stack of two square flues linked by a round arch and balustrade. From the rear this can be seen to be raised on two arches. In renaissance revival style, it is of squared stone with ashlar dressings and slate roofs throughout. The single storey L-shaped infants' school has Flemish gables and retains its arched covered play yard. The junior school, rectangular with a projecting short rear wing, is of two storeys, also with Flemish gables both large and small; these have triangular and rounded pediments respectively. Ground floor windows have arched tops. The original gates and walls survive, with the inscriptions on the gate piers marking the segregated boys' and girls' entrances; the railings are modern. Much altered in the 20th century, but the internal layout remains close to the original.

The school sits between late Victorian and Edwardian suburban development and 1930s housing. Disused since 2008, when the community centre which succeeded the school was closed, it is sadly empty and vulnerable.

Brightside Board School
Jenkin Road S9 1AS
1880 and 1882, E R Robson
Listed Grade 2

The second of the two schools commissioned by the Board from E R Robson. Brightside in 1880 was a small, isolated settlement either side of the Midland Railway line and above the steadily expanding steelworks of the Don Valley. The area now contains light industry and housing of a variety of ages.

Brightside is an early example of the School Board thinking beyond the provision solely of teaching space; a central hall was also provided, notwithstanding Robson's original reluctance on cost grounds - he thought Whitehall would not agree. Nevertheless the school came in at £12,600 and an eventual per capita cost, for 908 places, of £13.6s 8d, below the Board's average. Robson's 1880 school, of 762 places, is E-shaped, of stone with the usual ashlar dressings, and differed significantly in appearance from the Board's previous schools. There are two storeys, the front elevation having five arched ground floor windows; above, three gables, again with tall arched windows with central traceried lights, the gables separated by smaller rectangular windows. The gable ends of the block are topped with a panel, segmented pediment and finial; they contain a central arched window and two side windows on each floor. In 1882 Robson added a Flemish Renaissance Revival nursery block; single-storey, H-plan and of 9 bays, it has an attic and dormer windows, and end gables pedimented to echo the main school, but with squared windows. The eyecatcher at Brightside is his extravagantly-styled caretaker's house, also of 1882, of 3 storeys and attic, with swept coped gables topped with pediments, square shafts and chimney stacks. It echoes some of Robson's London schools, and is a marked contrast with the simplicity of the 1880 structure; what stimulated this?

Brightside: the caretaker's house © Mary Howson

Woodside Board School

Rutland Road S3 3PB
1880 and 1881, Innocent and Brown; 1895, C J Innocent

© Ainscough

By 1880 Innocent and Brown's schools had become simpler. English Domestic Gothic was not abandoned as an overall approach, but the detailing was less complex. Woodside School demonstrated this change.

Construction was of rock-faced Walkley stone and Grenoside ashlar, the roofs of dark Westmoreland slate with red ridge tiles. Inside, the roofs were partly open-timbered; all rooms had pitched pine dados. Passages, cloakrooms, stairs and lavatories were lined with glazed bricks.

Accommodation was initially for 310 juniors and 332 infants. The extensions raised total capacity to 1046 and added the caretaker's house. The original plan to provide separate blocks for boys and girls was not achieved until 1895. Meanwhile the upper floor of the initial block was used for both boys and girls, the main schoolroom being divisible by a glazed sliding partition. Glazed partitions between all the rooms gave the head teacher a commanding view of the school. All rooms had open fireplaces in addition to a hot water heating system. Ventilation was via upright inlet tubes, with outlets in the ceiling connected to a main extraction shaft.

The site was not ideal for the Board but it could not find a better location in the district. Other local schools were grossly overcrowded and such was the pressure that Woodside was not fully equipped on the day of opening, as the ship carrying castings for the desks was wrecked on her voyage from Glasgow to Newcastle. The roads in the neighbourhood were unfinished and the Board petitioned the authorities to repair them as they were considered dangerous to the children.

Woodside was closed in the late 1960s and later demolished.

Burgoyne Road Board School

Burgoyne Road and Cundy Street S6 3QF
1881, Innocent and Brown; 1889, C J Innocent

Opened in 1881, this was Innocent and Brown's last joint commission (Brown died in 1881). Built for 934, it was extended in 1889 to 1224; at under £11 per place it was one of the most economical of the Board's schools. It was a local authority school until 1975. In 1978 St Mary's Church Primary School moved into the Cundy Street side of the premises, which it still occupies. In the late 1990s the rest was refurbished as apartments.

Both buildings are of cream stone with grey slate roofs and red ridge tiles. The two storey block on Burgoyne Road has 4 arched windows above a stone string course, one arch now extended as an entrance to apartments; rectangular windows above, with shouldered stone lintels. A cross-wing extends behind. Another, larger range stretches across the site. Plain in design, it is of 2 and 3 storeys, on the slope of the hill, with the caretaker's house tucked in on the lowest level. The window pattern resembles that of the two-storey block, with mainly arched windows to the lower floors of the east elevation and the first floor of the end wall. The north, Cundy Street elevation has a double gable with a big arched recessed window in each; between, twin chimney stacks join at the top to form a bellcote, its stonework forming a cross very like that at Langsett Road. A projecting wing at the rear has a diagonally-placed chimney stack; of two storeys, it is built out from the down-slope, over an arched passageway. Beyond it is a single-storey extension block.

The original boundary walls and some inscribed gateposts survive, as do some walls segregating the play areas, and some original railings. An open sided roofed play yard retains its cast iron columns.

Duchess Road Board School
Duchess Road S2
1883 and 1889, C J Innocent

Mr Leyland's Class, Duchess Road School, 1910

This was Innocent's first Sheffield school commission after the death of Thomas Brown. The design featured classrooms radiating off a central hall from the end of which the headmaster's platform commanded the entire school. Solid wooden block floors made a noiseless surface for, eventually, 1024 pupils - infants, junior and secondary.

The main, Tudor-style block, of Walkley stone with Grenoside ashlar dressings, had two storeys under a black Westmoreland slate roof surmounted by a large well proportioned flèche serving as a bell and ventilation turret. The upper walls of the classrooms were plastered, with pitch pine boarding below, but with glazed sections onto the hall. Lower walls in the hall and corridors were covered in white and buff glazed bricks. The usual playgrounds were supplied with drinking fountains. Heating was by steam on the Leeds patent system installed by Longdon & Co, Sheffield. Ventilation was by fresh air inlet tubes with regulating valves and by Boyle's patent exhaust ventilators.

Duchess Road was one of the schools first chosen to provide handicraft centres for the teaching of woodwork for boys, equipped with the aid of local manufacturers. It was also chosen for teaching practice when the teacher training college attached to Firth College became a reality in 1890. The buildings suffered extensive damage during the blitz in World War II. Closed in 1940, the school re-opened as an infants' school in 1948, but was closed in 1982 and later demolished.

Huntsmans Gardens Board School
Attercliffe S9
1884, C J Innocent

The school, on a sloping site, was named after the nearby building in which Benjamin Huntsman invented the process of cast steel in 1773. This was an area in the east end of Sheffield, of heavy industry with a rapidly expanding population living in high density terraced housing. Built of coursed stone and dark Westmorland slate at a cost of £16,270, it accommodated 1,250 pupils, boys, girls and infants.

Innocent here developed further the approach to layout he had used at Duchess Road. The plan was effectively a panopticon, the central hall being a semi-circle with a headmaster's desk on the straight side. 12 galleried classrooms (three behind the headmaster) were divided by movable partitions allowing flexible use of space and accommodation for varying numbers of pupils. The classrooms were square to accommodate equal length desks, and mostly lit from the left. Electric bells were fitted by J. Northam & Co Sheffield, enabling the Head to summon teachers, or the caretaker from his house.

The main building was single storey at one end and two storeys lower down the slope. An extensive gymnasium was included in the lower part, accessible by steps from both the boys' and the girls' areas. Infants were placed in a separate building with a schoolroom and four classrooms. Heating throughout was by a low pressure steam system. Lavatories were provided with patent closets. The three asphalted playgrounds were surrounded by sturdy walls, with covered play sheds, and drinking fountains; clearly, pupil welfare was taken very seriously.

The school was closed in 1980 following housing clearance, and subsequently demolished.

Sharrow Lane Board School
South View Road S7 8AE
1887, 1890 and 1894, C J Innocent

Sharrow began as an elementary school, accommodating senior children. Infants' and junior departments were soon added and by 1894 it had places for over 1000 children. It is now a community centre.

Innocent designed the whole, in the usual cream stone with decorative ridge tiles on the slate roofs. There were the usual separate entrances and playgrounds for infants and girls (on the east side) and boys (on the west). By Innocent's standards the school is decidedly simple, lacking his earlier trademarks except for the covered play area; this survives intact, with open arches on three sides and narrow buttresses between them. Cast iron columns support a flat ceiling with stout timber beams. Above was the infants' school: small dormer gables top large rectangular windows, with narrower windows alongside, all under stone lintels. On the east elevation these are curved on the lower edge, and incised. One gable here contains 'SBS' in stout stone lettering; the usual date and cartouche are absent.

The main range is on two floors, with large central gables on the south side, and smaller, barge-boarded gables (one set back) either side of them. Windows on the ground floor are round-arched, but rectangular above. A clumsy link with the infants' school is relieved only by an elegant column supporting the porch roof. Ashlar string courses and lintels throughout, with ashlar banding also in the gables. In the north-west corner of the site are the later junior department and caretaker's house, much altered.

Why was this school so different from Innocent's earlier work? The budget was doubtless tighter. It is however difficult to avoid the thought that in designing the main range, Innocent was trying out something much closer to E R Robson's style.

Owler Lane Board School
Owler Lane S4
1889, Wightman and Wightman; 1901, W H Hale; 1911, F E P Edwards

A 600 place elementary school, its close proximity to Grimesthorpe Board School (whose own capacity was being increased as Owler Lane was building) says much about local population density and growth. Owler Lane itself was extended in 1901 and 1911, to accommodate a total of 1240 children.

This was the first of Wightman and Wightman's two schools for the Sheffield Board and their building, which cost £20,000, was squarely in the style well-established by the Board. Hale had begun taking commissions from the Board in 1896, but Owler Lane seems to have been his first for an extension rather than a complete school. The two-storey rectangular, many-gabled 1911 building was a good deal plainer and more workaday in appearance. F E P Edwards who built this had become the City Architect in 1908; his work included the Dr John Worrall School in Attercliffe (1915) and most notably the 1914-1923 extension to Mountfield's 1897 Town Hall.

The school was closed and demolished in the early 1990s. A bell turret and the door heads of the Boys' and Girls' departments are preserved on an open space near the site.

Abbeydale Board School
Abbeydale Road S7 1RB
1890, 1893-4, 1895, C J Innocent

Built at the very edge of the Board's area, to relieve pressure on other schools, this elementary school was for 885 children; a planned extension in 1895 brought capacity to 1622. Innocent's design was even simpler than at Sharrow Lane, on which he was working at much the same time. The *Sheffield Independent*, reporting the opening, drew a fair picture of the first building: 'The principal front of the building faces the main road, and it is two stories high, with gables and large windows, with no unnecessary ornament. Coursed wallstone is used on all sides of the school, with ashlar dressings, and the best Westmoreland slates. Pitched pine is applied to all interior woodwork........Block flooring is laid, to minimise sound, and the whole of the interior is abundantly lighted and ventilated.....'. The layout gave the headteacher a full view of everything that was going on, and classes could enter and leave without crossing others.

The first building was in fact of 3 storeys, the upper two with boys' classrooms on the first floor, girls' above. Its two large gables frame a recessed central frontage; between, roof dormers have simple barge-boards. First and second floor windows are rectangular, those below are arched; there are carved crosses in the top floor lintels. Some elegant door-lintels and ironwork. Two chimney stacks form a bell turret. The 1895 infants' school, behind the first, also has 3 storeys, and an integrated caretaker's house. In 1890 the School Board approved the installation of glass-lined water pipes as the original lead pipes were thought dangerous; it is unclear whether any other Board school was similarly treated.

Abbeydale's original walls and gateposts survive, with excellent lettering denoting the girls' and boys' gates. It is now a Nursery, Infant and Junior School.

Carlisle Street Board School
Carlisle Street S4 7QX
1891, H E Hodgson and J E Benton; 1894, J E Benton

A detailed image of the school has not been found; this view just shows the school (in the middle ground on the left) from Petre Street, looking over the Munitions Street huts in Grimesthorpe. These were built during the First World War as temporary accommodation for munitions workers and converted into family housing afterwards. Children from this estate no doubt attended the school, which is dwarfed by works chimneys and almost totally lost in the choking smoky haze from the Atlas and Norfolk Steel works.

Designed by H. E. Hodgson of Sheffield, the construction supervised by J E Benton, the style was said to be 'Elizabethan' and the total cost was £14,871. Each of the two storeys had two large departments and four classrooms with cloakrooms; the ground floor was for girls, the upper for boys. Classrooms were divided from the main school by glazed panels. The corridors and staircases were lined with glazed bricks to a height of 5 feet. The building was heated by hot water on a low pressure system and ventilation was secured by means of air pumps. Each playground had a covered shed.

Catering for 750 pupils when built, with Benton's extension of 1894 it accommodated a precise 1121 pupils, 360 boys, 360 girls and 401 infants. The extension provided a main schoolroom, a further three classrooms, cloakrooms, a marching and play corridor, mistresses' rooms and a lavatory.

The school was closed and demolished many years ago, but a substantial length of its boundary walls survives on Carlisle Street East.

Neepsend Board School

Hoyland Road S3 8AB
1890, J B Mitchell-Withers

© Ainscough

Built on a hill above the bank of the River Don, in a heavily industrialised area of Sheffield, Neepsend School occupied about an acre and a half of land north of the city centre.

Standing above the large Clifton Steelworks, the school was surrounded by rolling mills, engineering works, iron foundries and back to back housing built around courts. In this none too salubrious district the school provided, according to a contemporary report, 'light, convenient and comfortable buildings attractive in appearance without being expensively treated with architectural adornments'.

Built in an English Renaissance style, of stone from the local Bole Hill quarries, with Grenoside dressings, Neepsend provided for 750 children, senior, junior and infants. The building boasted Flemish gables and a bell turret. Boys were accommodated on the ground floor which contained one large and four smaller classrooms partitioned off from the main room and each other by glazed partitions. Girls' classrooms were on the first floor, no doubt to a similar layout. Lavatories, a cloakroom and teachers' room were incorporated into the design. Internally, floors were wood blocks, the internal woodwork pitch pine with cement dadoes.

The school closed in 1958 and was subsequently demolished.

Heeley Board School
Anns Road S2 3DJ
1890-92 and 1899, C J Innocent
Listed Grade 2

This became the largest of the Sheffield Board's schools, eventually accommodating 1656 pupils, and the most expensive in total - over £21,606 by the time it was finished. Its cost per head was nevertheless below average. It opened in 1892 with 1206 places; in 1899 60 more were added for Infants and a girls' block (for 390) with cookery room was opened. The latter was among the facilities shared with other local schools, as was the metalwork room for boys. Between 1896 and 1905 the school also provided evening classes for pupils aged 12-21 who had not had elementary education.

It is an especially good and complete example of C J Innocent's later, solo work. The style is renaissance revival, in stone with ashlar dressings and gabled and hipped slate roofs, with decorative ridge tiles and finials. There are three main blocks, all substantial. The 1890 nursery at the west corner is single storey and double range. It has an octagonal louvred wooden bell turret with ogee lead dome and finials, and the gables have the Board's name inscribed, surrounded by lush stone foliage. Indeed, the detailing is all fine.

The infants' and primary blocks are of two storeys plus basement, with an octagonal stair turret. The gables retain their ball finials and the roof its two octagonal cupolas. There is a caretaker's house, which with the original perimeter walls and separate gates for boys, girls and infants survive. This was Innocent's last commission for the Sheffield Board.

The school closed in 2006, when a new school building to the north of the original buildings was opened. It remains empty and has been subject to some vandalism, including the breaking of windows and the loss of some of the roofing.

Woodbourn Road Board School

Woodbourn Road, S9 3LQ
1892, Wightman and Wightman, and Edward Holmes

© Philip Wright

The school was begun by Wightman and Wightman but after the death of the firm's remaining partner was completed by Edward Holmes (who later with his partner A F Watson built several more Sheffield schools). One of the Board's larger schools, catering for 1224 pupils and with one building for infants and another for older boys and girls, it cost £15,500. On rising ground above the Don Valley, the two-storey elementary school is at the top of the sloping site. In two ranges with a transept section, it is of honey-coloured coursed stone with ashlar dressings; the roof has a bell turret, its original cross finial now gone. The style tends towards the Gothic but the design is much simpler than, for example, those of Innocent and Brown. The main, south-facing elevation has 2 large gables and 2 dormers each topped by a trefoil pedestal. The infants' department was single-storey, in line with then current theory; it provided 360 places. In both buildings the central of the three windows within each gable is arch-topped.

The caretaker's house and the boundary walls, capped with rough triangular stones, survive; so do the playsheds, one for each school, that for the elementary school retaining its cast-iron pillars.

The school later became a middle school but was closed in 1982, following a decline in local population which originally served the nearby collieries and works. It is now in community use as a Pakistani Muslim centre.

Hunter's Bar Board School
Sharrow Vale Road S11 8GZ
1893, C J Innocent; 1906-7, A F Watson

Hunter's Bar was, the Leopold Street schools apart, the Board's most expensive school in terms of cost per place, at over £24 against an average £14.

Originally for 360 pupils, an extension was later required and the Education Committee commissioned a second building, opened in 1907, to add 760 places. By this time terraced housing was spreading beyond Hunter's Bar towards Ecclesall. The site on rising ground gives the school a commanding appearance, emphasised by the high walls and stepped entrances on the north side. The gateposts retain some of their original labels.

Both buildings are of stone. Innocent's school is 1 and 1 ½ storeys, with a church-like projecting porch. Dated 1892 and with the Board's initials beneath a stone shell carved on an end gable, it has an attractive central tower with pyramidal roof, weather vane, decorative fake machicolations and an octagonal chimney to one side. The tower makes a neat connection between the wings. The 1 ½ storey wing has pointed-arch ground floor windows - was this once an open play area? The gables have decorative finials and striking decorative carving around some windows; a small circular dormer window with keystone and bands is labelled 'boys' above the original entrance now obscured by a modern addition. The roof has witch's-cap openings for ventilation shafts.

The 1906 extension is dated on the rainwater heads. A simple 2 ½ storey block, its bottom floor arched windows are divided by buttresses. The rectangular windows above are under stone lintels topped with quite elaborate crosses. Fine Arts and Crafts lettering is used for the door labels, for boys, girls and 'Manual' , the last denoting the addition of technical education facilities.

Hunters Bar is now an infant and junior school.

Firshill Board School
Barnsley Road S3 9AN
1893, J B Mitchell-Withers; 1906, J R Wigful

In what was then a middle-class late Victorian suburb of detached and semi-detached housing, many of whose occupants petitioned against its establishment, this has always been, as it remains, a primary school. Built for 848 pupils, and costing over £11,000, it is a T-shaped, 2 and 3-storey Jacobean style block of coursed stone and slate roof, its rectangular windows dominating each elevation and separated by buttresses with champfered copings level with the top of each storey. The first floor windows, triplet in form, fill the spaces beneath the gables; over each window is not only a lintel but a sill above, creating a very 'square' impression. On the Barnsley Road elevation are two curved Jacobean gables, on the back three triangular gables. In the stem of the 'T' a slightly projecting feature contains an elegant main entrance; smaller, rather meanly-scaled doors for the pupils are crowded into the ground floor.

In 1906 J R Wigful added a caretaker's house and an additional school building behind the main school, in Orphanage Road. This is single-storey and very plain in appearance, but with a distinctly Arts and Crafts style bellcote on the main roof ridge. Wigful copied the triplet window design of Mitchell-Withers' school and the stone sills above the lintels of the central of the triplet. This building was presumably dedicated to infants' classes; the surviving gateposts are signed accordingly.

Some of the original boundary walls remain, but the railings are modern replacements. There are numerous modern extensions. The school was used as a 150-bed military hospital in WW1.

Bole Hill Board School
Bole Hill Road S6 5DD
1896, W J Hale
Listed Grade 2

An imposing structure set high above the Rivelin Valley – and exposed to Pennine weather – the excellent external condition of Hale's monumental school is tribute to the quality of both design and materials. This was his first new school commission for the Board, though he had handled the Owler Lane extension in 1899.

Bole Hill provided 815 places in a single block. Of rock-faced stone, its high slate roof features a prominent octagonal bell turret; the lower stage is of stone, the upper two of wood, each with louvres. The main range is double, with a cross range to the south-west end and a small cross-extension at the rear to the south-east. 2½ storey, with a third storey at one end. There are 5 bays, the 3 in the centre beneath small triangular gables with finials. Buttresses, capped at each level, flank the central bay. The basement windows are stone-arched. To the south-east, the front range ends in a prominent flat-topped gable with finial; to the south-west, the back range has three storeys, with two small, quite elaborate stepped gables and beneath the string course some Celtic-style carved decoration. A small projecting structure has a swept, coped parapet.

The south-west cross-range announces the Board's ownership in a elaborate stone tablet, the Board's name set against foliage, all placed high in a stepped gable; beneath it, a large arched first floor window with keystones.

The separate caretaker's house is tall and narrow, under a prominent stepped gable enclosing the second floor window. The two open playsheds with cast-iron columns supporting the roofs have been enclosed. Some original walls and inscribed gateposts survive.

The building has been in community use for some years.

Tinsley Park Road (Coleridge Road) Board School
Tinsley Park Road, S9 5DL
1896 and 1903, Holmes and Watson
Listed Grade 2

Tinsley Park Road school opened in 1896 with 760 places; the 1903 school, alongside, was for a further 750 senior pupils. The caretaker's house was added at the same time. The school was renamed Coleridge Road in 1912. The area was then dense with housing; when this disappeared, the 1896 building became redundant and was later demolished. The surviving building is a specialist education centre, surrounded by industrial premises (though housing is reappearing not far away).

The handsome structure that survives fully justifies its G2 listing. Of cream stone in Renaissance Revival style, its double height central hall has ramped, shouldered Flemish gables with a central pedestal and urn finial linked to the keystone of the large round-arched window beneath. Its roof has two pagoda-like octagonal wooden turrets with tall finials and glass panels. The single-storey classroom ranges surround the hall; rather simpler, but still elegant. There is a projecting cross-wing. The classrooms feature distinctive and elegant convex and concave coped gables, the larger over triple rectangular windows. The separate boys' and girls' doors are marked in stone.

The 1903 caretaker's house is two-storey, with moulded cornice and cartouche linked to the string course and a square, shallow bay window and a further cartouche in a triangular stone frame at the bottom of the roof gable. The original coped boundary walls and inscribed gateposts survive intact, as do the boundary walls of the 1896 building.

The school was designed to the latest thinking on elementary schools. There was an innovative heating and ventilating system which the Board's Chairman thought essential 'for the welfare of the children in these dark and smoky districts. The school should be made as cheerful as possible'.

Pomona Street Board School
Pomona Street S11 8JN
1900, Holmes and Watson

Opened in 1900 as a 590-place elementary school to serve the population expanding south from the city centre, the school cost £13,000. The Board had wanted to build in the area from the late 1880s; it was opposed by local residents and private education interests, and under pressure from Whitehall, Springfield School was extended instead. Eventually a further school was unavoidable and Pomona Street was erected on the open land proposed for it over a decade earlier.

The regular form of the school was made possible by the unusual (in Sheffield) level site. Rectangular, 3 storeyed, except for a 2-storeyed front section, of coursed stone and slate roofed, it has 3 elaborate bell turrets along the main roof ridge. The centre of the north front has six bays of tall windows on each of two floors beneath a large gable with what Pevsner's *Sheffield City Guide* describes as 'strangely Mannerist-shaped parapets' bearing ball finials, and 'buttresses that turn into pilasters above the ground floor'. Between the lower six windows are cartouches with carved flowers, one bearing the date 1899. The frontage either side of the central section contains at first floor level a pair of tall, recessed windows with arched stone lintels. Beneath them are lintels with stylised carvings and a central bud-shaped finial, and there is another pair of tall windows on the ground floor below. Beyond them, again on each side, three smaller rectangular windows on each floor; between the two levels another, small window topped with triangular pediments. It makes for a rather restless composition.

The return elevations are simpler with plain rectangular windows; the rear elevation has two plain string courses between the floors and two more 'Mannerist' gables. The original boundary walls are intact.

The school is now Porter Croft Primary School.

Upperthorpe Board School
Daniel Hill Street S6 3JH
1900, Hemsoll and Paterson; 1907, Patterson

Upperthorpe Elementary School opened in 1900. In later years it was known as Upperthorpe Nursery, First and Middle School; in 1992 it became Daniel Hill Primary School.

The schools served a late Victorian residential suburb, of mostly lower middle class terraced housing clinging to steep slopes. It was the first of the three built by Hemsoll and Paterson for the Board. It cost £12,675, including the caretaker's house, and accommodated 810 pupils. Paterson was responsible for the extension of 1907 for the City Council.

As was common there were two separate buildings, both of cream stone with slate roofs. The earliest, at the bottom of the site, was for 810 pupils; single storey, in an extended H shape, it had a central bell cote. Paterson's 1907 school, further up the hill, added 400 infant places, and facilities for manual instruction and cookery. It had a double range of 2 and 2 ½ storeys. On the main elevations simple Flemish gables, some topped with curved pediments, enclosed large rectangular windows, many triplets and with decorative lintels; there were smaller paired arched windows elsewhere. On the playground side, the slope of the hill allowed the construction of arches which formed covered play areas; they were later filled in to create extra accommodation.

The buildings, including the caretaker's house which stood on the boundary wall between the main buildings, were demolished after closure in 1999. Some boundary walls survive, with gateposts marked 'Girls' and 'Infants'. The site is now occupied by residential development.

Western Road Board School
Western Road S10 1NE
1901-3, 1904, Holmes and Watson

Built as Crookes was expanding, but the Board again planned ahead; even in 1905 there was open land on two sides of the site, and Crookes had not altogether lost its village character. The Board bequeathed two substantial buildings and a caretaker's house, at a relatively high £20 per place. Their 'arts and crafts' feel signals the architects' later progression to Nether Green and Carterknowle schools. The elementary school on Western Road is handsome, with simple but elegant Flemish gables pointing up the eight classrooms surrounding a high-roofed central hall. The long elevations almost match, but on Western Road the central gable rises to a decoratively carved bell turret supported on pilasters. At each end of this facade, small wings have triangular gables and sweeping roofs. The hall roof has 2 louvred ventilators under domed turrets. Detailing throughout is careful and good.

The adjacent single-storey infants' school is similar in style, a double range with Flemish gables on every side. Those facing the playground bear floral carved inscriptions contained in stone sills above the windows – SEC, for the Education Committee, and 1903 – though this building had been planned by the Board.

Facing on to Mona Road is the 1904 addition; a much simpler affair, a long range of 1 ½ storeys, with rectangular windows with stone arched segments above, and two triangular gable ends onto the road. It added places for a further 440 children.

On Western Road the boundary walls and elegant gate pillars survive; most of the former open playsheds are now filled in. There are the usual internal playground walls, for segregating boys, girls and infants. The school is now Westways Primary.

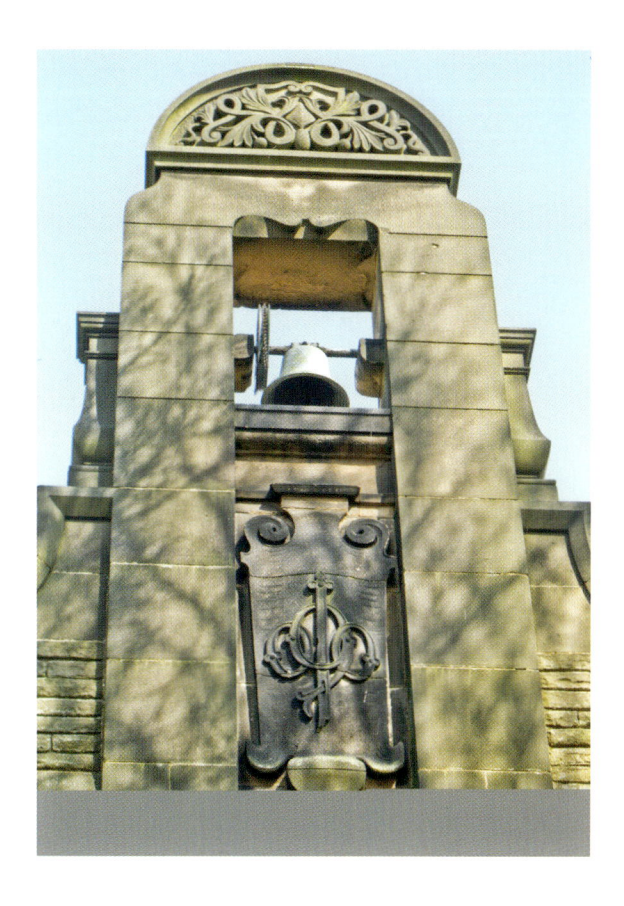

Morley Street Board School
Morley Street S6 2PL
1901, Hemsoll and Paterson

What is now Rivelin Primary School was built for 810, at a cost of £14,600. Its two buildings are of rock-faced stone with ashlar dressings, but there are some architectural differences.

A 3 storey block faces Morley Street; a double range, each of 4 bays, the 2 central ones topped with shouldered gables above second floor windows which are arched-topped twin lancets flanked by smaller rectangles. The flanking bays have triple lights, the central one single arch-topped and topped by small Dutch gables. Between the first and second floors a simple incised inscription bears the Board's initials, the school's name and the 1901 date. At each end a stair tower is set back from the main frontage, an arched window at the top set under a shouldered parapet. The rear facade has a single central gable in the projecting central section.

The second block, at the rear of the site, has 2 storeys, with third floor attic rooms in the gables at either end of building. The gables have a string course above the first floor. The centre is brought forward as a substantial bay with a Dutch gable, enclosing the arched central window, set in a curved slate roof. Substantial stone lintels top the ground floor windows; the upper windows have a mix of lintels and stone arches.

Like other late Board schools, Morley Street offered specialist facilities, reflected in the doors marked 'Cookery School, Girls' and 'Manual Instruction, Boys'.

The caretaker's house is of the same stone, square with a slate roof and ashlar band between the floors, and a stone bay window on the street elevation. It has been heavily modernised. The original stone walls in Morley Street remain, as do some inscribed gateposts, but the railings are modern.

Ranmoor Council School

Fulwood Road S10 3QA
1904, Holmes and Watson; 1909, A F Watson
Listed Grade 2

Originally an elementary school, Ranmoor has the distinction of being the first school opened by Sheffield Education Committee, though commissioned by the School Board before its demise.

One of Sheffield's few Arts and Crafts schools, Ranmoor features the striking roof lines often associated with that style. Of Bole Hill stone and Matlock ashlar, it has an asymmetrical front elevation featuring two Flemish gables with 3-light windows, the central one topped with a stone arch and keystones; pilasters rising between the windows terminate in the capped gable shoulders. Behind the front range rises a large central hall with a big end gable and arched window; the round-arched bell turret above has a circular opening, now empty. Square towers with louvred openings, quoins and moulded copings flank the end gable. 1 and 2-storey side wings are recessed from the front. Inside, the queen post truss hall roof survives.

The most interesting of Holmes and Watson's schools, in plan it echoes earlier schools which grouped their classrooms round a central schoolroom. Eight of the proposed eleven classrooms were built in the first phase, the three to the south being later additions. The schoolroom could be divided into two classrooms by a timber and glass screen, but the head teacher could still see across both. The classrooms were designed so that light fell from the left hand side of the pupils' desks. The playgrounds offered drinking water fountains, and the centenary history also mentions pencil sharpeners there. The high cost of £14,100, including the caretaker's house and boundary walls, reflects the difficulties of building on the site.

The building was taken over by the War Office in 1915 for use as a military hospital. It is now Nether Green junior school.

Greystones Council School
Tullibardine Road S11 7GL
1904, Hemsoll & Paterson, extended 1914

Greystones was designed by Hemsoll and Paterson and completed by Paterson after Hemsoll's death in December 1903.

The 1904 building, of rock-faced stone from Bole Hill, with ashlar dressings from Stoke quarries, has a large hall with classrooms off it. The usual glazed screens were provided to divide the classes, and the hall itself. Internally, many original features remain, notably the wooden beams supporting the hall roof, glazed partitions to the classrooms and some elegant moulded doorframes. Externally, there are stylish swept gables framing the classroom windows. The rainwater heads drain from circular openings between the gables, the openings featuring keystones at the top and mock ones at the bottom. The hall has three arched traceried windows in the end gable. At one end of the roof, a substantial Flemish gable rises to a two-staged bell turret beneath a dome. Single storey, with two-storey corner blocks with an Arts and Crafts flavour.

The 1914 building, planned from 1911, provided an infants' department for 400 on the upper of two floors, with its own entrance. Beneath were facilities for medical inspections, cookery and laundry instruction (a doorway marked 'Domestic Subjects' survives). Of simple appearance, it has circular windows in the tops of the gables on the Tullibardine Road side, each with a keystone at the top and a mock one below. Beneath the shouldered gables, triple-light windows are topped with stone arches. The rainwater heads, emerging from the tops of buttresses between the gables, are dated 1914. Internally, the classrooms led off a central hallway.

The caretaker's house of 1904 and most of the boundary walls survive. In the 1930s and 1960s three smaller buildings were added.

Interior of 1904 building © Anita Chib

Hammerton Street Council School

Ouseburn Road S9 3AA
1904, W J Hale
Listed Grade 2

A Council school, commissioned by the School Board before its abolition, and known at different times as Ouseburn Road School and Kettlebridge School.

Opened in October 1904 and costing £14,000, the school catered for 340 infant and 540 junior pupils from an area of housing contemporary with the school. Much of this remains, supplemented by modern development, but the school was closed in 1994. After a long period of neglect and vandalism, it is now owned by an educational trust and restoration has begun with a view to returning it to school use.

W J Hale was an important provincial architect based in Sheffield; this school is widely regarded as his best building. Of mellow Bole Hill stone, with Stoke ashlar dressings and roofed in Westmoreland slate, it is the best Arts and Crafts school in Sheffield. The infants' department, now demolished, contained six classrooms off a central corridor. The surviving junior school grouped nine classrooms round a central schoolroom with moveable glazed partitions. The exterior is characterised by coped gables with squared, flat-topped buttresses; many windows have elaborate elongated lintels. The main doors feature ornate key stones and bow-fronted cornices. Some of the original decorative drainpipes survive, topped with arches and keystones. The central hall is high and hipped-roofed, with clerestory windows; at each end is a narrow tower of two stages with openings on the longer sides. A notable feature is the set of wreathed cartouches on three sides of the building, at the top of the buttresses and in the gables. Each is carved with the name of a virtue to be instilled, presumably, by the education provided: Courage, Bravery and Courtesy round the boys' entrance, Purity, Sincerity and Modesty around the girls', with Justice, Truth, Grace and Honour along the front of the school. Some elegantly-carved gateposts survive.

Malin Bridge Council School
Dykes Lane S6 4RH
1904, H I Potter; 1910, Potter and Sandford

The school was built for 800 pupils; the extension raised capacity to 1200. The 1904 range, of rock faced stone with some ashlar dressings, has 2½ storeys facing down Meredith Road. It is symmetrical with four gables on this side. Windows are rectangular and topped with stone arches. At first floor level the central bays have more elaborate arching over the middle of three lancet windows. Each of the two central gables carries a very prominent stone label – unique among Sheffield schools - bearing the school's name and date, and beneath each label a large keystone rising from the window arch. Rising from the roof behind these gables a tall octagonal domed turret - probably a ventilation tower – has patterned lead covering. The rear elevation to the playground has three gables, the row flanked by buttresses. The original perimeter walls survive on this side, with good Arts and Crafts lettering for the gatepost inscriptions. There are covered playgrounds.

Facing Dykes Lane is the single storey addition of 1910, with three main bays and smaller extensions. Plain in appearance, it has tall rectangular windows with stone lintels and mullions. Behind rises the hall, with large arches in the end gables, filled with herring-bone stone around surprisingly small arched windows.

In Norris Road, but within the school's curtilage, is the caretaker's house; a small, detached stone house with deep sloping roof, tall chimney and shouldered gable at each end.

Woodseats Council School
Chesterfield Road S8 0SB
1905 and 1909, H.L Paterson

Built of stone in a very simplified English Domestic Gothic style. The infants' school, for 340, was opened in 1905. A single storey triple range, its main gable ends face the road; beneath the gables, 3-part windows, the middle part higher and topped with arched dripstone mouldings. On the roof is an attractive square ventilator with Doric columns supporting a dome, and a bellcote complete with bell rising from a large gable with an arched window beneath.

The 1909 junior school, for 840, is at right angles to the infants'. Of two storeys, and plainer in style – though with minor 'arts and crafts' touches – it has asymmetrical facades. On the south, three large gables with triplet windows reflect the classrooms within, and are flanked by taller through-eaves windows beneath stone arches with keystones. On the north are one large gable and three smaller arched, shouldered ones. The caretaker's house between the two blocks, and the boundary wall and gates, survive; the walls much lower than in earlier schools, as fashion changed. There was careful segregation of pupils, with the boys' entrance on the far side of the site, leading off The Dale, and the girls' and infants' combined gate, still clearly visible, on the Chesterfield Road end of the 1909 block, although the boys' door has been obscured by a modern extension. The interior has been much altered.

Woodseats only became administratively part of Sheffield in 1901. A still-expanding suburb of working class and lower middle class terraced houses, shops and workshops, with a number of quarries and a brickworks, it bordered on open fields, long since gone; but the school is still a school, Woodseats Primary.

Carterknowle Council School

Carterknowle Road S7 2DY
1906, Holmes and Watson
Listed Grade 2

An Arts and Crafts school, of rather busy appearance. A single building of now darkened cream stone with a slate roof, it is H shaped, with a central hall surrounded by classroom ranges, mostly single-storey but on the east side having a substantial semi-basement with classrooms lit by large arched windows separated by buttresses. The long elevations in Carterknowle and Fossdale Roads are matching. Small, projecting, two storey wings at the west and east ends house the doors. Over the doors are handsome carved labels denoting the boys' and girls' entrances. Each main elevation has three Dutch gables, the central one large, enclosing rectangular windows. The projecting wings do not match; the north one has a plain gable topped with a pediment, the south a shouldered arched gable. The west projecting wing on the Fossdale Road side has stone arches on the ground floor which appear to have been filled in; presumably these began life as a covered play area.

The roof has interesting features: twin octagonal turrets topped with louvred ventilators, a central domed turret, a gabled bell turret complete with bell, and numerous gable windows through the eaves.

The original boundary walls and railings survive, as do the elegant gateposts with the original characteristically arts and crafts lettering. The caretaker's house, two storeys plus attic and also in arts and crafts style, is in the corner of the grounds. Originally a 700-place elementary school and now for junior pupils, Carterknowle notes that efforts have been made to preserve original features, 'both externally and internally'.

Wadsley Bridge Council School
Penistone Road North, S6
1906

A single-storey school serving the population of an expanding industrial area round Wadsley Bridge. There were two simply-designed stone buildings, fronting on to Penistone Road. The main range had a large central gable flanked by smaller ones, all containing rectangular windows, and there were small symmetrical projecting blocks at each end. The large hall, surrounded by classrooms, had clerestorey windows. Originally an elementary school, it was for a period a special school and later became Sheffield Council's Beeley Wood Training Centre. It stood on the east side of Halifax Road, just north of the railway bridge. The building was demolished in 1997 and the site is now in commercial use.

Highfield Special Council School
Sitwell Road S7 1BG
1907, A F Watson

© Valerie Bayliss

The Sheffield School Board decided just before it was abolished in 1903 to purchase land in Sitwell Street, 'for any of the......purposes' of a school which might be, in the terminology of the time, 'for defective children, a cookery centre, and a centre for manual instruction'. In the event, the building designed by Alfred Watson and opened in 1907 was at first what would now be called a special school. From an early stage it offered three departments: a centre for teaching 80 children with learning disabities on the ground floor, and rooms for teaching manual subjects and cookery on the upper floor. These served visiting pupils of other local schools. All of the Board's options thus came to fruition. Later it was used as a mainstream girls' high school (whose signboard remains in situ). It ceased to be a school in 1986, and has been used latterly as a youth centre.

The building, erected for the City Council, is small, of the usual cream stone. Of two storeys, it has two large gables on each of the east and west elevations. A substantial Dutch gable on the south side is sadly obscured by a large, later extension with its own roof which sits cross-wise to the main structure. Windows are rectangular throughout. The slate roof is topped by a bellcote, but the bell has gone. Elegant stone walls and gateposts survive on the Sitwell Road boundary. The building is now used as a youth centre.

Lydgate Lane Council School
Lydgate Lane S10 5FQ
1907, W J Hale

Crosspool began to be built up from the 1880s and the Education Committee opened this school on high ground on the edge of existing areas of early Edwardian housing. The structure and carvings remain in excellent condition; the stone, a fine gritstone widely used in West Sheffield, almost certainly came from Bole Hill or Bell Hagg quarries.

After Hammerton Street, Hale continued in Arts and Crafts style here. This is however no copy but a distinctive design which survives largely unaltered. The single building has two prominent gables in its main, south-west elevation, inscribed 'Sheffield Education Committee Lydgate Lane School 1907'. The two-storey-high pilasters alongside have flat capstones, as at Hammerton Street each inscribed with a curricular virtue - 'Honour', 'Courage', 'Courtesy', 'Reverence' etc. The arched upper floor windows between the pilasters have long keystones. Between the large gables is a pair of smaller but similarly-styled gables, again with buttresses. All the gables are triangular. The cross-ranges facing Lydgate Lane contain the main doors, that on the north-east in a projecting porch, both topped and flanked in ashlar features with prominent capped pilasters. The south-east entrance (now obscured by a modern porch) sits beneath a small gabled window rising from the door surround. Between the cross-ranges is a curved gable-top. The north-east facade has three gables in the same style as those on the south. On the roof, an octagonal open bell-turret has a domed cap, the lower part with patterned covering.

The original walls and elegant gateposts, with their inscriptions, remain. So does the caretaker's house, with its tall distinctive chimneys matching those of the school. Lydgate Lane is now an infants' school.

Salmon Pastures Council School
Warren Street S4 7WT
1908, Smith and Ensor

When the Lord Mayor opened the school in 1909 he called it 'the last word in elementary school building'. It took over three years to build, and at £18,700 was expensive; the cost included special asphalt and concreting in the foundations to prevent waterlogging during flooding, as the site was close to the River Don. Moreover there was a special mechanical heating and ventilation system, the latter a complete reversal of any used before. All the doors and windows were made to shut tightly and the air was washed in two huge hollow coconut fibre drums, then conveyed into the school through an extensive system of ducts. *"In this way the dirt of Attercliffe is triumphantly set at nought and the atmosphere of the school constantly kept pure and undefiled".* The Lord Mayor remarked in his opening speech that those condemned to live amid the smoke of the big industrial works should have everything possible done for them by the city in the provision of amenities.

The main building was fairly simple but substantial, with a Dutch gable facing the street and some arts-and-crafts style decorative features. It had specialised accommodation for handicrafts (for boys) and cookery (for girls) and was the first to have a fully-equipped laundry room, again for girls.

The building was damaged by enemy action in the Second World War and by 1942 was no longer in use. It was later used by Parkwood College but demolished in 1998. Its stone sign is preserved on the Five Weirs Walk.

Whitby Road Council School

Fisher Lane, S9 4RP
1909, Potter and Sandford

© Philip Wright

Opened in 1909 for 810 pupils, at an economical cost of £4762. The area was up the hill from the Don Valley steel works, and housing developed here from around 1903. The school site was opposite the Craven Railway Carriage and Waggon Works. It now houses Greenlands Nursery First and Greenlands Junior Schools.

From the outset the site contained two separate schools in separate buildings, for junior and infant classes. The junior school, fronting on to Fisher Lane, reared above the terraces of housing which extended almost to the school walls. It has two storeys, built of coursed stone under a slate roof; the original bell turret has been removed. Rectangular, with stair turrets and simple, shallow buttresses. Windows are tall and mainly plain in design, but on the main elevation two triangular gables surmount triplet windows each of them capped with a pointed arch and tall keystone. On the south, Staniforth Road side there are five triangular gables again with triple windows, the central one being double. There were separate entrances for boys and girls; the inscriptions survive.

The separate infant school faces on to Whitby Road. It is single-storey but the natural fall of the land permitted an extensive cellar which was used to provide baths and washing facilities for local people. E-shaped, with two large end triangular gables and smaller gables facing Whitby Road. The central strut of the E was the school hall, and was partly hexagonal. This building retains its bell turret.

The caretaker's house survives, heavily modernised.

High Wincobank Council School
Bracken Road S5 6FH
1908, G.A. Wilson

The school was built to meet the rising demand from families living in the new Flowers Estate, which had been developed on a previously unoccupied area of farmland. The secondary school, for 912 pupils, was an imposing 2 and 2 ½ storey structure, dominating its corner site, its appearance was very different from most of Sheffield's board schools, not least because unlike virtually all Sheffield's other schools up to that date it was built of brick. The main elevation had six gables, alternating large and small, with 3 windows in each gable; irregular roof line. Each floor had a large hall surrounded on 3 sides by classrooms, the senior children using the upper floor with juniors below. Alongside was the single-storey, double-range primary school, also of brick.

The school was requisitioned as a military hospital in 1915. The schools were closed and the buildings demolished in the mid-1990s.

Ellesmere Road Council School
Maxwell Street S4 7JN
1913, F E P Edwards

The city architect was responsible for this large school, which also absorbed the two next-door Methodist School buildings which were substantially refurbished for school use. They survive, and are in use respectively as a Hindu community centre (in Maxwell Street) and a children's centre (in Ellesmere Road). The brick-built school itself, however, was demolished over a decade ago and its site is now covered by modern housing. All that remains is the 1913 caretaker's house, a 2 storey building, red brick below and stucco above, reminiscent of the nearby Flower Estate and other early Sheffield council housing.

The Township Schools

Sheffield's boundaries have been extended several times since 1870, so some schools built between 1870 and 1914 by the school boards of Ecclesfield, Handsworth, Eckington and Mosborough, Beighton and Norton were incorporated into the city. Boundary extension in 1901 brought five Norton and Ecclesfield schools under the Sheffield Board. When all school boards were abolished in 1903 the remaining township schools became council schools in the West Riding or Derbyshire, depending on location; some of these were subsequently absorbed by Sheffield through further boundary changes from 1921 onwards. This section looks at a selection of the surviving schools which began as township schools, in predominantly rural areas, but ended up in the city.

Ecclesfield School Board

Established in 1882, by 1902 it had built a creditable seven schools. Hillsborough and Low Wincobank opened in 1884, Grenoside and Burncross in 1885, Ecclesfield in 1894, Chapeltown Warren in 1900 and Lound in 1901. Hillsborough and Low Wincobank became Sheffield schools in 1901, the remainder transferring from the West Riding in 1974. Hillsborough, Low Wincobank and Lound are still schools. Grenoside currently stands empty. Burncross, Ecclesfield and Chapeltown Warren have been demolished.

The Ecclesfield schools, and their subsequent enlargements, had a recognisable architectural style, and they were all built of stone. They were all designed by George Archibald Wilson (of the practice Wilson and Masters 1876-1887).

Hillsborough Board School

Parkside Road S6 2AA
1884, G A Wilson/Wilson and Masters; 1892
Listed Grade 2

The school was opened as a 250 place infants' school and 350 place elementary school in the triangle bounded by Parkside Road, Catch Bar Lane and Leppings Lane. There was then relatively little housing nearby, but the opening of Hillsborough Park and the arrival of the electric tram in 1901 brought rapid housing development. In 1892 a separate girls' department was added, in the east building, and a further building appeared on Catch Bar Lane a few years later. All four buildings have similar designs and are largely unaltered. In 1901, when 1320 pupils were recorded, the Sheffield City boundary extension brought the school within the city.

Wilson's design was in his single storey 'cottage' style, adopted for most of the Ecclesfield Board Schools. The junior school has slightly projecting end gables and a central gable containing the entrance door. Between the gables are pairs of mullioned windows. The gables are the most characteristic feature of Wilson's schools; each has timber barge boards topped by a terra cotta 'egg cup' finial, most of which survive. Below the bargeboard is an almost semi-circular gothic window surround. Recessed slightly are the mullioned and transomed windows; the upper transoms have scalloped decoration, and the curves above are filled with herring-bone patterned stonework. Rising from the ridge line above the central gable is an ornate ventilator and bell turret with a tapering slate-clad spire and topped by a weather vane. Most of the Ecclesfield schools had this feature, but this is the only one to survive.

The adjacent infant school was doubled in width early in the twentieth century. The school had a caretaker's house on Leppings Lane, dated 1884; a headmaster's house was added in Parkside Road during the 1890s.

Wincobank Board School

Newman Road S9 1LU
1884 and 1894, Wilson and Masters; 1907, G A Wilson

Wincobank opened in 1884 for 360 pupils. Situated on rising ground backing on to Wincobank Hill, it was west of the village, then mostly of terraced houses. The original building was T-shaped with a six-bay frontage to Newman Road, the larger end bays being gabled and set forward. An extension in similar style was added to the rear in 1894 and at the same time the west gable was extended forward to the pavement line, bringing the total capacity to 528 pupils. The usual segregation of boys and girls was observed in the separate entrances: the boys' on the east side, the girls' and infants' at the front.

The school has many barge-boards, all topped by 'egg-cup' finials. Below the gables are the typical gothic mullion and transom windows which were Wilson's trademarks. Wincobank is nevertheless simpler in design than, say, Hillsborough.

The grounds were enlarged in the later 20th century, a play area being added to complement the modest playground surrounding the school buildings. Most of the original boundary walls, with coped gatestones, survive.

Norton School Board

The Board was formed in 1872 and began its building programme in the face of local opposition. It erected three schools, Norton (now Mundella), Meersbrook Bank and Bradway, and acquired two existing schools, Greenhill National School and Cammell's School at Woodseats. Greenhill was extended in 1877 and 1890. Norton, Meersbrook Bank and Cammell's passed to the Sheffield School Board with the boundary extension of 1900 ('Norton Within'). Bradway and Greenhill passed to Derbyshire County Council until the Sheffield boundary extension of 1934 as did the just-begun Norton Lees('Norton Without'). T H Wilson was the architect to the Board until 1895.

Norton Board School
Mundella Place S8 8SJ
1875 and 1893, T H Wilson

Wilson's 700 place infants' school opened in 1875, at a cost of £2700, on a site procured from the Duke of Norfolk for £375. This rather plain school has been much altered and extended.

The 1875 range facing Mundella Place is a long, single-storey stone building with a projecting gable at the east end incorporating a Tudor-style window with a cusped triangular gothic opening above. The remaining thirteen windows are now largely obscured by a brick extension of the 1930's which badly compromises the front elevation. The school contained two large rooms and two classrooms. The largest room, holding 400, was needed for boys and the other large room, adapted for 300, was devoted to girls. The classrooms could be adjusted if needed to accommodate 50 children each.

The 1893 extension, for 250 pupils, was at right angles to the first building. Its street gable, at the west end of the main frontage, balances the 1875 eastern gable and has similar detailing. Most of the 1893 extension was however demolished in the late 1930's, to be replaced by a larger brick building catering for the children from the many semi-detached houses that now surround the school. A further new building of c. 2000, fronting Derbyshire Lane, has replaced a row of houses.

The school was transferred to the Sheffield School Board in 1901. It remains in use as a junior and infants' school, named after Anthony John Mundella (1825-1897), a Sheffield MP for nearly 30 years. A promoter of the 1870 Education Act, Mundella improved on it with his own Act of 1881 when he was Vice President of the Council of Education.

Meersbrook Bank Board School
Derbyshire Lane S8 9EH
1894, T H Wilson; 1899, Joseph Norton

Little fanfare was raised by the local press when the Norton School Board's new school was opened in 1894, at a cost of £4050. On a steep slope between Binfield Road and Derbyshire Lane, it was in a rapidly expanding area in the Norton district of Derbyshire. Housing and industry had spread along the main route from Sheffield to Chesterfield, following the line of the railway into a previously agricultural area. The single building, the architect's best design, has two parallel ranges; a central gable, set slightly forward, faces the street and rises to a bell turret. Within the gable is one of T H Wilson's characteristic tripartite Tudor-style windows; over it the Board placed its name and the date, beneath a triangular gothic opening. Plainer wings extend either side.

In 1899 a much larger Junior School was added, in very different style. An austere 2 ½ - 3 storey edifice of local stone, with Dunford Bridge facings and Grenoside dressings, Meersbrook Bank school was a squat T in shape, with three storeys at the front and two at the rear. It has a full-height central gable topped by a chimney stack and flanked by several smaller gables. The lower floor has four segmental arched openings, possibly originally giving access to a covered play area. The ten classrooms, some with folding partitions, each had dual desks for sixty children. The basement had enclosed play sheds. The walls and railings of both buildings survive.

The school transferred to the Sheffield Board in 1901. The Board purchased a dwelling house and outbuildings adjacent to the school for use as a caretaker's house. It remains in use as a Junior and Infants school.

Bradway Board School
Bradway Road S17 4QS
1903

This modest school building was opened in 1903 by the Norton School Board, whose name and date of establishment are recorded at the top of the central raised coped gable to the road elevation; this also features a carving of the Chantrey Memorial Obelisk built on Norton Green in 1854. The remainder of the triangle has a chequered pattern of alternating stone blocks and herringbone brick, a pattern repeated on the gable ends. The school is a small, plain stone building with a slate roof topped by decorative ridge tiles above which rises a pair of tapering stone chimneys with the still surviving bell mounted between. In the school yard the original open play shed, supported on iron columns, survives.

The building is now in community use, including a pre-school nursery.

Norton Lees Council School

Argyle Close S8 9HJ
1903, Joseph Norton; 1913
Listed Grade 2

Responsibility for Norton Lees was much transferred during its development. It was designed by Joseph Norton for the Norton School Board, which commenced its building in response to extreme pressure of numbers on existing school places. Sheffield's boundary extension of 1900 swallowed up the area, the Norton School Board was dissolved and the building was completed by the Sheffield Board at the very end of its life. But it opened in 1903 under the aegis of the new Sheffield Education Committee. Sheffield School Board had nevertheless asserted its role by fixing its name and crest to a gable.

Described at its formal opening as a "handsome business-looking pile standing on the side of a hill well out of reach of the smoke of the city", it is indeed a massive structure. Norton Lees met the needs of a growing suburb. It accommodated 980 pupils (360 mixed juniors, 360 mixed seniors and 260 infants) in three buildings, a two-storey block for the juniors and another for the seniors, and a single storey block at the rear for the infants. Each section had a large schoolroom and four classrooms, furnished with dual desks. Ceilings were 14 feet high to ensure good ventilation. As was common, two of the classrooms on each floor could be combined with the main schoolroom by use of sliding partitions to create a large open space. The lavatory provision was lavish by contemporary standards: 27 WCs and 20 hand basins.

The caretaker's house and boundary walls survive, as does a relative rarity, the playground shelter at the rear. All these are listed, along with the school buildings themselves.

Norton Lees was renamed Carfield School in 1924 and has borne that name ever since.

Eckington and Mosborough School Board

This Board began in 1871 and soon found itself running 5 schools, but only one, Halfway School, later became a Sheffield school.

Halfway Board School
Station Road, S20 3GU
1877

The school opened in 1877 with only 70 pupils on roll, though it seems to have been built for 200 boys and girls and 80 infants. By 1889 there were 300 pupils, 80 of them infants, but in 1912 total numbers were only around 280.

The stone-built Eckington and Mosborough School Board building was, and in appearance remains, a typical village school, of one storey with symmetrical gabled wings, beneath steep slate roofs, joined by a central section. The gables contain blank stone circles and beneath them rectangular mullioned windows beneath small open pediments. The cross-range windows have elegant lintels. The original boys' door retains its stone label under a drip moulding. On one side elevation, a substantial chimney stack bearing in a stone niche the Board's arms, badly eroded; perhaps it had the date at one time. Some original walls survive, as do the ornate main gateposts, topped with ball finials. It may not be accidental that these mark the way in to the headmaster's house, a substantial two-floor dwelling in Elizabethan style.

Taken over by Derbyshire after school board abolition, the school was subsequently brought within Sheffield's boundary.

Handsworth School Board

The Board appointed John Dodsley Webster as its architect (he had been unsuccessful in seeking the Sheffield Board appointment). A number of Handsworth schools later transferred to Sheffield, either directly or via a period in the hands of West Riding or Derbyshire county councils. Not all the buildings survive: Woodhouse West (1900) and Woodhouse Secondary Council, later Woodhouse Grammar (1909) have been demolished, as has Handsworth School, Fitzalan Road (though its boundary walls still surround the empty site). Woodhouse East Board is no longer a school, but remains in education use as a training centre; Normanton Springs has been converted to housing. Intake (1884) and Gleadless (1898) schools continue in that role.

Intake Board School
Mansfield Road S12 2AR
1884, 1892, J D Webster; 1911

The first building was a single storey school, of village school character, probably of T shape with projecting shouldered gables at each end and a gabled front door. The northern gable carries prominently the name of the Handsworth School Board and the opening date, 1884. Of cream stone, with mullioned windows and ashlar dressings, some in red stone – these apparently random in distribution, so a puzzle. The gable windows are cusp-topped and sit beneath dripstones placed beneath stone arches with herringbone infill. The big rear wings running back from the front range, of stone and in broadly matching style, are probably Webster's 1892 extension. The substantial master's or caretaker's house, possibly also of 1892, is integrated with the front range.

A further large extension was provided, as a mixed school, in 1911; this is the L-shaped brick building behind the original school. Its opening left the older school as accommodation for the infants' department.

Intake was taken over by West Riding County Council when the Handsworth Board was abolished in 1902; it was absorbed by Sheffield in 1921. The school is now Intake Primary School.

Woodhouse East Board School
Station Road, S13 7QH
1889, J D Webster

Opened in 1889 by the Handsworth School Board. Of coursed stone, 2 ½ storeys and on a plinth, the front elevation is symmetrical. The two end wings are brought forward to present large gables containing triple-light windows on each floor, the central lights in the upper floor rising slightly higher. All are topped with stone blank arches. The main gables, and the through dormer gables on the front, have ornamental finials. In the recessed portion of the front are three doors, of which one is contained in a stone arch with keystone; of the others, the central door looks like a later insert. The remains of a wall bellcote survive above the east door. To the rear and sides, symmetrical and rather severe elevations with dressed ashlar string courses.

The school came within West Riding County Council from 1903 and transferred to Sheffield in 1921.

Gleadless Board School

Hollinsend Road, S12 2EJ
1898, J D Webster

When it was built, the area was largely agricultural, and the school not that far from Intake school; so where did the children come from? Most of the surrounding housing development dates from the 1930s. Nevertheless, the Handsworth School Board decided to borrow the money to build it from the Prudential Assurance Company, at 3 ¼ % over 30 years. The architect's estimate of £3600, which he could not explain, was thought high – 75% more than the Board had spent at Woodhouse – although local Fox Wood stone from Intake was to be used. One consequence of the high cost was the Board's decision to abandon the provision of a caretaker's house.

The school is a quite substantial, coursed-stone building with a capacity when it opened of 440. Symmetrical, and of two storeys, its stepped front gables enclose three large windows on each floor. The main roof has witch's cap ventilators. The rear elevation is simpler, with string course and a slightly projecting centre. Modern additions have not dealt kindly with Webster's design.

The school transferred from West Riding County Council to Sheffield in 1921.

Beighton School Board

This board appears to have built only one school, and that eventually came within Sheffield.

Beighton Board School
School Road S20 IEG
1880, 1896

The board's only school, it was opened in 1880 for 500 pupils, and there was an endowment for ten free scholars (parents were at this date still required to pay a fee). In 1896 it was enlarged to take 836 pupils.

A substantial building in creamy-yellow stone, and of one and two storeys; originally single-storey, the school's website tells us the first floor was added in 1896. The gables frame large windows with segment-headed lights, and above them small circular recesses, some glazed. The ground floor windows, and those on the side elevations, are rectangular. The main door sits in a slight one-storey forward projection; it has above it an ornate stone panel of ivy leaves, with a blank shield, and containing the Board's name; beneath, on the door lintel, are the two construction dates.

The caretaker's house is alongside, and the original low front walls survive.

Appendix

Sheffield Schools and their architects, 1870-1914

Dates are of opening

C J Innocent and T Brown

Newhall, Sanderson Street, 1873
Broomhill, Beech Hill Road, 1873
Netherthorpe, Netherthorpe Street, 1873
Philadelphia, West Don Street, 1873
Attercliffe, Baldwin Street, 1874
Carbrook, Attercliffe Common, 1874
Crookesmoor, Tay Street, 1874
Lowfield, London Road, 1874
Walkley, Greaves Street, 1874
Darnall, Darnall Road, 1875
Park, Norwich Street, 1875
Grimesthorpe, Earl Marshall Road, 1875
Pye Bank, Andover Street, 1875
Springfield, Broomspring Lane, 1875
Manor, Manor Lane, 1877
Fulwood, David Lane, 1878
Langsett Road, Burton Street, 1879
Woodside, Rutland Road, 1880
Burgoyne Road, 1881

C J Innocent

Duchess Road, 1883
Huntsman's Gardens, 1884
Sharrow Lane, 1887
Abbeydale, Abbeydale Road, 1890
Gleadless Road, 1892
Hunters Bar, 1893

T Flockton and E R Robson

Firth College, Leopold Street, 1879
School Board Offices, Leopold Street, 1879
Central Schools, Orchard Lane, 1880

ER Robson
Heeley Bank, 1880
Brightside, Jenkin Road, 1880

H W Lockwood
Teachers' Centre, Holly Street, 1899

Wightman and Wightman
Owler Lane, 1899
Woodbourn Road, 1892

Hodgson and Benton
Carlisle Street, 1891

J B Mitchell-Withers
Neepsend, Hoyland Road, 1891
Firshill, Barnsley Road, 1893
Central Schools, Orchard Lane, extension, 1895
Bow Street, 1894

W J Hale
Bole Hill, Bolehill Road, 1896
Hammerton Street, 1904
Lydgate Lane, 1907

Holmes and Watson
Tinsley Park Road, 1896
Pomona Street, 1900
Western Road, 1901
Ranmoor, Fulwood Road, 1904
Carterknowle Road, 1906

Hemsoll and Paterson
Upperthorpe, Daniel Hill Street, 1900
Morley Street, 1901
Greystones, Greystones Road, 1904

H L Paterson
Woodseats, Chesterfield Road, 1905

H I Potter
Malin Bridge, Dykes Lane, 1905

T H Wilson
Norton, Derbyshire Lane, 1875
Meersbrook, Derbyshire Lane, 1894

Wilson and Masters
Hillsborough, Parkside Road, 1884
Low Wincobank, Newman Road, 1884

Joseph Norton
Norton Lees, Argyle Road, 1903

A F Watson
Highfields Special School, Sitwell Road, 1907

Smith and Ensor
Attercliffe, Salmon Pastures, 1904

Potter and Sandford
Darnall, Whitby Road, 1909

G A Wilson
High Wincobank, Bracken Road, 1910

F E P Edwards
Ellesmere Road, 1913

J D Webster
Gleadless, Hollinsend Road, 1898
Woodhouse East, Station Road, 1889
Woodhouse West, Sheffield Road, 1900

Select Bibliography

Barnes, S F: *Manchester Board Schools 1870-1902*. London, The Victorian Society, 2009

Bingham, J H: *The Sheffield School Board, 1870-1903*. Sheffield, J W Northend Ltd, 1949

English Heritage: *Revised List of Buildings of Special Architectural or Historic Interest: City of Sheffield*. English Heritage, 1995

Hague, G: *The Education Department Offices, Central Schools and Firth College*. Typescript, Sheffield Local Studies Library, 1990

Harman, R and Minnis, J: *Pevsner Architectural Guide to Sheffield*. Yale University Press, New Haven and London, 2004

Harwood, E: *England's Schools-History, Architecture and Adaptation*. Swindon, English Heritage, 2010

Innocent, C J and Brown, T: *Illustrations of public elementary schools erected for the Sheffield School Board*. Sheffield, 1873

Leader, J: *Surveyors and Architects of the Past in Sheffield*. In *Lectures Read Before the Sheffield Society of Architects*, 1903

Mercer, S: *Schooling for the Poorer Child: Elementary Education in Sheffield 1560-1902*. Sheffield Academic Press, 1996

Seaborne, M and Rowe, R: *The English School; Its Architecture and Organisation. Vol 11, 1870-1970*. London, Routledge and Kegan Paul, 1977

Sheffield School Board: *Handbook of Information for Board Members, 1903*

Sheffield City Council: *Handbooks of Information for Education Committee Members, 1904-1915*

Welsh, S: *Biographical Notes on Sheffield Architects and their firms*, including W J Hale, S F B Holmes, C J Innocent, W Flockton, J B Mitchell Withers, J D Webster, J G Weightman. Typescripts, Sheffield Local Studies Library, various dates

Welsh, S: *A brief history of the important schools designed by private architects for the Sheffield school board and the Sheffield education committee between 1870 and 1910*. 1963

Wilkinson, E: *Broomhill School, 1873-1998*. Sheffield, 1998

Acknowledgements

This book is the product of a group but not of a committee. The research and writing were undertaken by Valerie Bayliss, Wendy Booth, Anita Chib, Susan Deal, Sue Freestone, Graham Hague, Judy Hague, Mary Howson, and Philip Wright. We are very grateful for the valuable support we have received throughout the project from the staff of Sheffield Local Studies Library.

We thank especially the Trustees of the Victorian Society for agreeing to provide financial support for publication from the legacy to the Society made by our late friend, colleague and South Yorkshire Group member, Jean Moulson, to whom this book is dedicated. We are also very pleased to acknowledge donations in Jean's memory from two Society members who wish to remain anonymous; these allowed us to commission professional photography.

We are grateful to Alex Ekins for the majority of the colour photographs in the book; many of these buildings, surrounded by walls and fences, are not easy to photograph. Thanks are due to Sheffield City Libraries for permission to reproduce images from www.picturesheffield.com; to www.copperbeechstudios.co.uk and David Ainscough for permission to use the photographs of Neepsend and Woodside Schools taken by the late Harry Ainscough; to Bryan Woodriff for the image of High Wincobank School from his collection; to Anita Chib, Mary Howson, Philip Wright and Valerie Bayliss for permission to use images in their copyright; and to Alistair Lofthouse and ALD Design and Print for publishing this book in partnership with the Society.

Numerous authors have provided information and guidance through their publications, which are listed in the select bibliography. In addition we are grateful to John Minnis, co-author of the Pevsner Architectural Guide to Sheffield, not only for pointing us to the topic of this book but for advice on our text. Any errors and omissions are of course the South Yorkshire Group's responsibility.

In the course of its work the Group amassed far more information, and many more images, than could be included in this volume. The images include in some cases new photographs of the interiors of some surviving schools. The additional material is being deposited in Sheffield's Local Studies Library where it will be available for consultation by anyone interested in learning more about Sheffield's Board and early Council schools.